Methods of changing behaviour

Andrée Liddell

Longman
London and New York

Longman Group UK Limited,
Longman House, Burnt Mill, Harlow,
Essex CM20 2JE, England
and Associated Companies throughout the world.

*Published in the United States of America
by Longman Inc., New York*

First published 1987

British Library Cataloguing in Publication Data

Liddell, Andrée
    Methods of changing behaviour. ————
    (Longman applied psychology)
    1. Behaviour modification
    I. Title
    153.8'5   BF637.B4

ISBN 0-582-29625-0

Library of Congress Cataloging in Publication Data

Liddell, Andrée
    Methods of changing behaviour.

    (Longman applied psychology)
    Bibliography: p.
    Includes index.
    1. Behavior modification.   I. Title.   II. Title:
Methods of changing behavior.   III. Series.
BF637.B4L53   1987   616.89'1   86-27642
ISBN 0-582-29625-0

Set in 9½ on 11pt Comp/Edit Times

Produced by Longman Group (FE) Limited
Printed in Hong Kong

Contents

Dedicated to the memory of my parents,
Lucienne and Albert Karch

Editor's preface

In most areas of applied psychology there is no shortage of hardback textbooks many hundreds of pages in length. They give a broad coverage of the total field but rarely in sufficient detail in any one topic area for undergraduates, particularly honours students. This is even more true for trainees and professionals in such areas as clinical psychology.

The Longman Applied Psychology series consists of authoritative short books each concerned with a specific aspect of applied psychology. The brief given to the authors of this series was to describe the current state of knowledge in the area, how that knowledge is applied to the solution of practical problems and what new developments of real-life relevance may be expected in the near future. The eleven books which have been commissioned so far are concerned mainly with clinical psychology, defined very broadly. Topics range from gambling to ageing and from the chemical control of behaviour to social factors in mental illness.

The books go into sufficient depth for the needs of students at all levels and professionals yet remain well within the grasp of the interested general reader. A number of groups will find their educational and professional needs or their personal interests met by this series: professional psychologists and those in training (clinical, educational, occupational, etc.); psychology undergraduates; under-graduate students in other disciplines which include aspects of applied psychology (e.g. social administration, sociology, management and particularly medicine); professionals and trainee professionals in fields outside psychology, but which draw on applications of psychology (doctors of all kinds, particularly psychiatrists and general practitioners, social workers, nurses, particularly psychiatric nurses, counsellors – such as school, vocational and marital, personnel managers).

Finally, members of the general public who have been introduced to a particular topic by the increasing number of well-informed and well-presented newspaper articles and television programmes will be able to follow it up and pursue it in more depth.

Philip Feldman

Acknowledgements

Grateful thanks are due to Graham Skanes and Chris Bilsbury who provided helpful comments on Chapters 1 and 2 respectively and David Hart who was always available to discuss the other parts. Pat Wall transcribed efficiently and cheerfully the case history and Cathy Butler carried out most of the secretarial work with intelligence and competence.

We are grateful to the following for permission to reproduce copyright material:

The Guilford Press for an adapted test from *Agoraphobia: Nature and Treatment* (1981) by Mathews, Gelder & Johnston; John Wiley & Sons Inc for fig 2.1 from fig 5.1 p120 by Meyer, Liddell & Lyons from *Handbook of Behavioral Assessment* ed. A. R. Ciminero et al. Copyright © 1977.

Chapter 1

The development of a technology for behaviour change

The implementation of treatment along behavioural lines is now considered orthodox practice. It is even the approach of choice with many problems, for instance, when dealing with mentally handicapped individuals, behaviour disordered children, or treating anxiety and phobic disorders. Behaviour therapy is well into its third decade and it has become part of the establishment. Hobbs (1964) claimed that, up to the time he wrote, there had been three mental health revolutions. Philippe Pinel in France, William Tuke in Britain, Benjamin Rush and Dorothea Lynde Dix in America were all associated with the first revolution, in that their shared concern for the humane treatment of mentally disturbed individuals heralded a dramatic change in the management of such individuals. Freud's focus on the intra-psychic life of the individual was central to the second revolution. The third mental health revolution is not so readily identifiable with any particular individual or individuals, but instead, it is identified with disparate innovations such as the therapeutic community, the open hospital, the increased interest in children and the growth of social psychiatry, all of which converged to make up the community mental health movement. Following Hobbs's reasoning, Levis (1970) labelled the growth of behaviour therapy as the fourth therapeutic revolution. This claim appears even more justified today.

The task of describing behaviour therapy was already daunting in the 1970s, in view of the enormous and unparalleled increase in the research and application of its techniques in clinical and non-clinical settings (Krasner 1971; Meyer & Liddell 1975). The growth has continued unabated and the task has become virtually impossible. Behaviour therapists are presently a variety of people who do not necessarily think the same way or do the same things with their clients and there is no simple definition which pleases every one of them. On the other hand, the changing definitions of behaviour therapy, although occasionally causing bewilderment, reflect a lively and progressive movement characterized by its unwillingness to remain static and be doctrinaire. The definition accepted by the Association for Advancement of Behavior Therapy in their *Guidelines for Choosing a Behavior Therapist* is also the definition which reflects the philosophy of this book and runs thus:

> Behavior therapy is a particular kind of therapy that involves the application of findings from behavioral science research to help individuals change in ways they would like to change. There is an emphasis in behavior therapy on checking upon how effective the therapy is by monitoring and evaluating the individual's progress. Most behaviorally-oriented therapists believe that the current environment is most important in affecting the person's present behavior. Early life experiences, long time intrapsychic conflicts, or the individual's personality structure are considered to be of less importance than what is happening in the person's life at the present time. The procedures used in behavior therapy are generally intended to improve the individual's self-control by expanding the person's skills, abilities, and independence.

Kazdin (1979) stressed the importance which behaviour therapy had for clinical psychology in strengthening the connection between experimental psychology and treatment. Clinical psychology in Great Britain, as well as in many countries where it is organized as a profession, remained peripheral in its contribution to mental health until there was widespread use of behavioural techniques in the management of psychological problems (Liddell 1983a). The behavioural approach is particularly amenable to research methodologies in which psychologists have expertise, giving treatment outcome research, in particular, a well-needed boost (see Ch. 7). Psychologist practitioners, heartened by the therapeutic success obtained with the new methods, gradually directed some of their efforts to reconceptualizing many of the problems which had previously been the province of psychiatry into psychological models capable of being refuted (Mathews, Gelder & Johnston 1981; Rachman 1978; Rachman & Hodgson 1980; Seligman 1975). While the development of behavioural psychotherapy is tied closely to the development of clinical psychology, the behavioural approach is by no means restricted to clinical psychologists. In fact, it has been taken up by psychiatrists and other medical practitioners, nurses, social workers, and physio-therapists, to name but a few. The many professional and learned societies or associations which aim to foster the responsible development of behaviour therapy are more often multi-disciplinary than restricted to a specific profes-sional group. Behaviour therapists with different professional backgrounds have contributed to the same scientific journals and these contributions have accelerated expansion of the movement to a variety of settings where professionals work together on the basis of a shared perspective (Marks, Connoly, Hallam & Philpott 1977). As well as expanding the domain of clinical psychology and psychiatry, the principles of behaviour modification have been applied in such diverse areas as child-rearing, education, medicine, paediatrics, gerontology, community work, criminology, business and industry. However, we should not lose sight of the fact that behaviour therapy first demonstrated its applicability with clinical populations and that, although narrow boundaries no longer hold, applications outside clinical psychology and psychiatry have not all reached similar stages in their development. For this reason and to confine the following discussions to manageable proportions, the focus of the book will be primarily on changing behaviour with clinical populations.

Behaviour therapy, behaviour modification or behavioural psychotherapy?

All of the above terms have been used earlier interchangeably and will continue to be used in this manner as equivalent terms. There have been instances when behaviour therapy and behaviour modification were given different connotations, particularly in the early phases of the development of the movement. Such distinctions were made on the basis of theoretical approaches, fields of applications, techniques used and countries where the application of learning techniques originated. For instance, behaviour modification has sometimes been thought to be a more generic term than behaviour therapy but it has been equally used in a narrower sense to denote the strict application of operant conditioning techniques. On the other hand, behaviour therapy was viewed by others as the more generic term or used in the narrow sense of referring to Wolpe's (1958) reciprocal inhibition technique for neurotic patients. However, distinctions of this sort have not been widely accepted and it is common practice to use behaviour therapy interchangeably in contemporary writings (Kazdin 1982a; Krasner 1982; Wilson 1978).

The British Association for Behavioural Psychotherapy was founded in 1972 and, at that time, there was a great deal of soul searching regarding an appropriate name for the new association. Behaviour therapy was seriously considered but came a close second in the end, perhaps because it was felt that there should not be a distinction between therapy and psychotherapy and that, in any case, *behavioural* is the feature which distinguished the approach from others. Since then, the name behavioural psychotherapy has been steadfastly identified with the British movement although there are occasionally some rumblings elsewhere (Editorial: Behavioural Psychotherapy 1983).

History

Eysenck (1959) first defined behaviour therapy as the application of modern learning theory to clinical disorders and the late 1950s are widely acknowledged to be seminal years in the development and acceptance of the movement. A brief history will be given from the early beginnings to the present day; more comprehensive histories are available elsewhere (Kazdin 1978a, 1982a; Krasner 1982).

It is possible to dig into the past for examples of treatment carried out on behavioural lines. After all, if the said techniques are based on principles which are demonstrated to alter behaviour, it is unlikely that observers of human behaviour living in previous ages were unable to make appropriate inferences and behave accordingly. Reports of precursors of behavioural techniques were reviewed by Kazdin (1982a), therefore only those influences within scientific psychology will be mentioned.

Mary Cover Jones (1924) is often quoted as one of the first behaviour therapists to report a single case study of a – now famous – child named Peter, using a technique akin to Wolpe's systematic desensitization. The child's phobic reactions to a rabbit were successfully changed when he used eating as a response incompatible with anxiety while gradually increasing the proximity of various types of rabbit stimuli. Other studies reporting the use of behavioural techniques, similar to those in current usage, are scattered in the relevant literature throughout the world. However, a more comprehensive picture emerges when one looks more broadly at the various streams of influences which converged together around the late 1950s and early 1960s to give impetus to the behavioural movement. (Krasner (1971, 1982) made a cogent analysis of these influences.) He listed as the first of them the acceptance of *behaviourism* within experimental psychology. The tenets of behaviourism were originally presented by J. B. Watson (1914, 1919) when he rejected consciousness as the domain of study of psychology. In its place he advocated the study of overt behaviour, in particular, the connection between various environmental stimuli (S) and the responses (R) which they evoked. This method of study became known as S-R psychology. His aim was to replace the introspective methods psychologists had introduced in the nineteenth century by objective methods such as the conditioned reflex method developed by Pavlov and other Russian psychologists. The concept of classical conditioning as the basis for explaining and changing normal and abnormal behaviour, along with research in instrumental conditioning, provided the original conceptual framework for testing learning theories. From the 1920s through the 1950s, various applications of conditioning and learning principles to human behaviour problems were carried out in the USA. In the UK, the general dissatisfaction with the psychoanalytic model and its influence on psychotherapy was primarily responsible for a group of researchers led by H. J. Eysenck elaborating therapeutic techniques based on learning principles and testing their efficacy against existing therapeutic methods. In 1950, the publication of a book entitled *Personality and Psychotherapy* by Dollard and Miller enhanced learning theory as a respectable basis for clinical practice. In this book the authors attempted to translate psychoanalysis into learning terms. The writings of psychologists such as Eysenck, Dollard and Miller were consistent with the philosophy of the clinical psychologist operating within the scientist-practitioner model, a philosophy which was clearly articulated and reaffirmed at formal conferences of the American Psychological Association, starting with the historic meeting held in 1949 at Boulder, Colorado. Meanwhile, in South Africa, Wolpe, an experimental psychiatrist, carried out research into the aetiology of neurotic behaviour with animals. On the basis of his findings he developed the technique of systematic desensitization with reciprocal inhibition for anxiety based disorders. In 1958, Wolpe published *Psychotherapy by Reciprocal Inhibition*, which was undoubtedly the most influential practical book of the period.

In addition to the influences already mentioned, work within some non-clinical areas of psychology, sociology and psychiatry also contributed to behavioural applications in the clinic. For instance, research by developmental psychologists regarding vicarious learning and modelling, the theoretical concepts and research studies of social role learning and interactionism in social psychology and sociology, social influence studies of demand characteristics, experimental bias, hypnosis and placebo responding captured the interest of clinicians. The new learning approach gradually provided a sound learning model as an alternative to the narrower disease model of human behaviour and the approach had echoes within psychiatry itself as it began to lean toward concepts of human interaction and environmental influences. Finally, it should not be lost sight of, that the period under scrutiny was a post-war era in which a better world was hoped for and it was thought that psychology and other behavioural sciences could be the basis for careful planning of the social environment to elicit and maintain the best of human behaviour. Such Utopian ideas were portrayed in *Walden Two* written by Skinner in 1948.

In his argument, Krasner (1982) stressed that the streams of development summarized earlier could not be viewed independently as they were continually in a process of interacting, changing and developing. Nevertheless, he was able to categorize the elements of the belief system common to behaviour therapy adherents thus: 'the statement of concepts so that they could be tested experimentally; the notion of the 'laboratory' as ranging from animal mazes through the basic human learning studies to hospitals, schoolrooms, homes, and the community; research as treatment and treatment as research; and an explicit strategy of therapy or change' (Krasner 1982 *Contemporary Behavior Therapy*, Guilford: 26).

Contemporary behaviour therapy

Concern has been expressed that the rapid increase in the application of behavioural techniques by psychologists and non-psychologists alike has given too little time for consolidation and adequate evaluation of the fast-spreading technology (Wilson & Franks 1982). Regarding the theoretical underpinning of behaviour therapy, critics outside as well as inside the movement were not slow to point out that there was no single unified learning theory and that links between research carried out in the laboratory and clinical practice were often tenuous. It was soon evident that simple learning principles alone could not be related to the effective processes found in the plethora of therapeutic methods described in the behavioural literature. As a result, it became obvious that complex human problems could not always be reduced to simple learning units, however appealing such reductionism had seemed in the past. Theories have therefore evolved and been modified to take account of observations gathered by clinicians. While there is no single theory which can accommodate all the technical know-how developed in recent years, efforts are continually made to test existing theories under the most rigorous scientific criteria. To bring some order to the contemporary scene, Wilson and Franks (1982) divided the movement into four main positions reflecting different standpoints, which they labelled the *four pillars* of contemporary behaviour therapy. Again it should be stressed that behaviour therapy does not exist in a vacuum and that it continues to be influenced by experimental psychology. Probably the most important of these influences on contemporary behaviour therapy is the rejection of a strict S-R position to permit the inclusion of cognition as a legitimate subject to study and the development of information processing models to investigate the subtleties of human thinking. The four major conceptual approaches of contemporary behaviour therapy are the following:

1 The neobehaviouristic (S-R) theory.

2 Applied behaviour analysis.
3 Cognitive behaviour therapy.
4 Social learning theory.

These approaches will be described briefly but for a more elaborate treatment than is possible here the reader is referred to Wilson and Franks (1982).

Neobehaviouristic (S-R) theory

The theory is considered to be an archetypal learning theory and closely identified with Eysenck who has worked systematically at verifying it for over thirty years. In Eysenck's words:

> The theory is labelled 'S-R' because, in a very real sense, it is the insistence on stimuli and responses that singles it out from other social and cognitive theories; yet this symbolism, too, is somewhat inaccurate. I have always argued, more than perhaps any other behaviourist, that the organism (O) intervenes vitally between stimuli and responses; indeed, it creates 'stimuli' from a welter of arbitrarily conjoined sensory impressions, and also creates 'responses' from a mish-mash of muscle twitches (Eysenck 1982 *Contemporary Behavior Therapy*, Guilford: 205).

Applied behaviour analysis

Eysenck's theory takes into account the intervention of individual characteristics between the stimulus and response and allows treatment to be focused upon aspects of behaviour such as anxiety which are not overtly seen but implied by certain responses such as avoidance. Applied behaviour analysts are quite different in their approach to behaviour change, in that mediational states, private events and cognition are strictly avoided by them. They draw primarily on the methodology of operant conditioning (Ayllon & Azrin 1968; Ayllon & Kelly 1972; Paul & Lentz 1977).

Cognitive behaviour therapy

This approach reflects the 'cognitization' of the main stream of experimental psychology. Unlike the other two approaches mentioned above, it stresses thought, beliefs and the assumption that people make their own environment. Cognitive behaviour therapists view maladaptive behaviour as resulting from faulty cognitions, replacing them with thoughts and self-statements that promote adaptive behaviour (Beck, Rush, Shaw & Emery 1979; Kendall & Hollon 1979; Meichenbaum 1977).

Social learning theory

In the past, many behaviour therapists have claimed an allegiance to a social learning approach, meaning simply that they were concerned with the effect of social and cultural variables on the behaviour of the individuals they observed. However, the orientation is best identified by the thinking and work of Bandura (1977) who took issue with the traditional assumptions that much complex and even simple behaviour should be attributed to rather direct connections between external cues and overt action. As an alternative to S-R psychology, he suggested that the lion's share of human behaviour was governed by cognitive processes which he described within an information processing model of thinking and behaving.

In a representative survey of behaviour therapy research published in the 1970s, Kendall, Plous and Kratochwill (1981) found that most respondents had been influenced by either applied behaviour analysis or social learning theory at the time the survey was carried out; far fewer respondents claimed to be affiliated with the neobehaviouristic (S-R) model or cognitive behaviour therapy. Since then, there has been an explosion in the application of cognitive behaviour therapy. New journals have been launched to provide outlets for the activities of groups of behaviour therapists who prefer to be known as 'cognitive behaviour therapists'. It also appears that the cognitive model most often tested is that of Bandura.

This book aims to describe the manner in which the behavioural approach is applied to clinical problems encountered primarily with adult clients. From the preceding sections, it follows that the approach is a broad spectrum one which draws from a wide range of experimental studies. It is hoped to demonstrate that clients are not rigidly managed with invariant techniques but are assessed and treated on an individual basis according to her/his need and want. Chronologically, assessing the nature of the problem is the first step leading to intervention; therefore the importance and complexity of this step will be covered in Chapter 2. Chapters 3, 4 and 5 will attempt to provide a practical guide to changing different categories of painful or undesirable ways of responding. The recent emphasis on teaching generalizable skills as opposed to well-defined skills to overcome specific problems will be the subject of Chapter 6. Chapter 7 will deal with various aspects of evaluating treatment outcome before final conclusions are drawn in Chapter 8.

Chapter 2

Assessment of problems to be changed

Behavioural assessment is central to behaviour therapy. A crucial difference between the behavioural approach to psychological problems and others is its emphasis on the continuous, rather than the discontinuous, links between normal and abnormal behaviour. In other words, abnormal behaviour is seen as maladaptive but influenced by the same laws which govern normal behaviour. In practice, it follows that abnormal behaviour can be assessed and treated directly, rather than conceived as symptomatic of some underlying and mysterious dynamic processes to be unravelled before treatment can proceed. Price (1978) described a number of competing approaches (including the learning perspective) to the understanding of abnormal behaviour and the reader is referred to his book *Abnormal Behavior: Perspective in Conflict* for a comparison between these various perspectives.

The most popular way of describing complex phenomena such as abnormal behaviour is in terms of a model. Models are in the nature of analogies which help scientists make sense of phenomena they wish to understand and control. For instance, problem behaviour has been conceptualized widely as an *illness*. Thinking of abnormal behaviour as if it were an illness has important implications. On the positive side it provided a workable framework for observation and categorization. It also made the subject matter part of a known discipline – medicine, or more specifically psychiatry. In general medicine, classifying diseases by their cause has changed it from an art to a science. Unfortunately, the aetiology of most so-called mental disorders is little understood, necessitating that different and less objective criteria be applied to establish a formal classification. Classifying abnormal behaviour has occupied many generations of psychiatrists since the end of the nineteenth century, when Emil Kraepelin, a German psychiatrist, established the basis of a broad schema which was to be modified several times to increase consistency and relevance to everyday practice. These modifications are currently the product of international collaborative efforts and the fruits of constant debate between representative practitioners. At the time of writing, practitioners in Britain, as well as many other countries, are able to use a commonly agreed classification of mental disorders issued by the World Health Organization (1978). The classification is part of the Ninth Revision of the International Classification of Diseases (ICD-9). In view of the difficulties encountered in classifying mental disorders, a glossary was introduced in 1968 and the following words of caution preceded ICD-9's glossary:

> The glossary in the mental health chapters of ICD-9, reproduced in this book is necessarily composed of descriptions of symptom patterns and syndromes rather than clear-cut or mutually exclusive definitions. This is because diagnosis by means of a few pathognomonic signs or symptoms is uncommon in psychiatry; in most instances, psychiatric disorders are differentiated from one another by the recognition of different patterns of emphasis among a comparatively small number of symptoms (WHO 1978: 10).

The American Psychiatric Association decided against using ICD-9, preferring to continue revising its own system on the grounds that a true consensus had not yet been achieved. In 1980, the most recent revision of the Diagnostic and Statistical Manual (DSM-III) of the APA was brought out for use. This third revision of the Manual introduced substantial changes, one of which was to classify individuals to be diagnosed on five axes rather than one. The American Psychiatric Association acknowledged the following definition of mental disorder:

> In DSM-III each of the mental disorders is conceptualized as a clinically significant behavioral or psychological syndrome or pattern that occurs in an individual and that is typically associated with either a painful symptom (distress) or impairment in one or more important areas of functioning (disability). In addition, there is an inference that there is a behavioral, psychological, or biological dysfunction, and that the disturbance is not only in the relationship between the individual and society. (When the disturbance is limited to a conflict between the individual and society, this may represent social deviance which may or may not by itself be commendable but is not in itself a mental disorder.) (American Psychiatric Association 1980: 6.)

 By way of conclusion, it appears evident from the above that both major psychiatric classification systems in current use had to modify the strict medical model to accommodate the various manifestations of abnormal behaviour. It should also be stressed that psychiatric classifications classify *disease*, which is an abstract concept, and not people. Unfortunately, disease labels accorded individual patients have often showed little prognostic value and have failed to predict the type of treatment ministered. Clinicians have need of a practical way of evaluating the many facets of their clients' functioning.

Origins of behavioural assessment

In her presidential address at the sixteenth annual convention of the Association for Advancement of Behavior Therapy, Nelson (1983) traced the origins of behavioural assessment to the late 1960s. The circumstances which favoured its development were the dissatisfaction with traditional methods of assessment and the pressing need of behaviour therapists to establish the effectiveness of their techniques. Behavioural assessment lagged somewhat behind behaviour therapy as a subject of study in its own right but there are presently a variety of good texts for those who wish a more comprehensive treatment of its nature and scope than is possible here (Barlow 1981; Ciminero, Calhoun & Adams 1977; Haynes 1978; Hersen & Bellack 1976, 1981).

Behaviour therapists, like other scientists, subscribe to a specified model to guide their interventions and the assessments which precede them. Nine basic assumptions regarding behavioural assessment were cogently identified by Haynes (1978). The following is a brief summary of these characteristics:

1 *A close association between assessment and intervention.* The interdependence of assessment and intervention is basic to behaviour therapy. The behaviour therapist initially works with his/her client to identify and specify targets for change along with an evaluation of the potential controlling and associated variables.

2 *Emphasis upon specification of variables.* Also fundamental to the behavioural control system and consistent with its empirical bias, is its emphasis upon precision and specification of all variables – be they target behaviours or environmental events. The first step in carrying out an analysis of behaviour is to focus on behavioural referents as opposed to vague, abstract, imprecise or non-behavioural ones. Antecedent and consequent variables (that is, what precedes and follows a behaviour of interest), must be identified before there is any attempt at change. The reliability and validity of the various behavioural measures and a true estimate of outcome depend on the degree of precision and specification made at the beginning.

3 *Emphasis upon quantification.* In addition to knowing whether or not a certain behaviour occurs and the

characteristics of that behaviour, it is desirable to know its frequency, duration and relationship to other behaviours. Counting, timing and measuring behaviour is not only useful to the therapist in selecting an appropriate intervention procedure, it also gives clients feedback, enhancing their self-understanding.

4   *Emphasis upon current environmental causality.* A major difference between the behavioural model and others is the assumption that a great degree of behavioural variance can be accounted for by current and historical environmental factors. However, it does not follow that behaviourists think that *all* behaviour can be accounted for by environmental factors. The part played by various neurological and metabolic factors is readily acknowledged. Increasingly, non-environmental factors such as physiological and cognitive ones are submitted to measurement and modification.

5   *Individual differences in behavioural characteristics and determinants.* Behavioural intervention programmes are usually individually worked out to fit the unique behaviour patterns and living conditions of individual clients. The assumption guiding behaviour therapists in the development of programmes is that differences exist between individuals necessitating an idiographic approach. Behavioural assessment derives some of its importance because it examines each case individually.

6   *Emphasis upon public events.* Public events are those which can be directly observed by other individuals with a high degree of reliability and with a minimum of inference. Examples of unobservable and inferential behaviour are feelings, attitudes, impulses, traits, needs, conflicts; *whenever* possible, these are avoided by behaviour therapists.

7   *Emphasis upon observation of behaviour in the natural environment.* Assessment in the natural environment is considered desirable for several reasons. It often reveals behaviour unreported during interview, or behaviour not evident from self-report instruments or laboratory observations. In other words, data derived from natural settings can be less inferential and biased than data derived from the clinic.

8   *Evaluation of assessment procedures.* Confidence in the results of behavioural assessment cannot exceed the validity of the measures used; therefore an important area of behavioural research is the continued development of relevant and accurate assessment procedures and furtherance of empirical investigation into currently used procedures.

9   *Behavioural therapy as a cybernetic system.* Haynes (1978) described a cybernetic system as 'one which, because of its construction, is self-assessing and, therefore, self-correcting and self-improving'. In this way, behaviour therapy is self-correcting and self-evaluating.

Behavioural interviews

In a recent revision of a widely used textbook on clinical psychology, Phares (1984) made the following comments regarding the assessment interview as used by clinicians:

... the assessment interview is at once the most basic and the most serviceable technique employed by the clinician. In the hands of a skilled clinician, its wide range of application and its adaptability make it a major instrument for clinical decision making, understanding and prediction. But for all this, we must not lose sight of the fact that the clinical utility of the interview can be not greater than the skill, care, and understanding of the clinician who employs this technique (Phares 1984 *Clinical Psychology Concepts Methods and Profession*, Dorsey: 177).

Meyer, Liddell and Lyons (1977) also defended interviews as an essential tool for the use of behaviour therapists and presented a schema for behavioural interviewing. There follows a discussion of the principles and practices of behavioural interviewing before an introduction to the more specific behavioural assessment techniques.

While the emphasis on precision, specification and quantification of public events is paramount to the philosophy of behaviourism, the behaviour therapist is also a clinician who needs to investigate the whole person before planning interventions. Simple reductionism of presenting problems needs to be supplemented at some point if the client is to leave the clinic as a whole person. It is believed that a multi-dimensional approach facilitates generalization of treatment effect and helps clients find appropriate ways of maintaining gains achieved under guidance. There is no single interviewing style which is deemed correct for every occasion. Interviewing is an interactive process between two people – the interviewer (therapist) and the interviewee (client) – each influencing and being influenced in turn by the other's responses. Some therapists have viewed the relationship between therapist and client as the most powerful ingredient contributing to change. Following from this, the conditions under which good client/therapist rapport develops, or more specifically how a good therapist behaves, have been widely investigated. It is now agreed that positive outcome cannot be attributed to therapist behaviour alone (Parloff, Waskow and Wolfe, 1978). On the other hand, much has been learned regarding effective interviewing tactics which can be applied in the clinic by clinicians of all persuasions.

Bernstein and Bernstein (1980) provided a helpful and comprehensive guide for health professionals who wish to develop their interviewing skills. They approached the interviewing situation in its totality and viewed interviews conducted by health professionals as a specific type of conversation in which professionals need to alter their more usual conversational patterns to a more disciplined style of communication. In their own words:

> He (the therapist) must assume responsibility for the conduct of the interview, but avoid the kind of control or rigidity that will inhibit or intimidate the patient and limit the patient's verbalization regarding the problem. The professional should keep content of the interview in focus while maintaining flexibility so that relevant material is not inadvertently excluded. He needs to remain sensitive to the patient's feelings, expressed both verbally and nonverbally, so that he can understand the relation of these feelings to the problem under discussion. His own subjective, personal feelings cannot be permitted expression in the professional situation. He must remain open and accepting toward his patient, sometimes even under the trying conditions of hostile, uncooperative behaviour (Bernstein & Bernstein 1980 *Interviewing: A Guide for Health Professionals*, Appleton-Century-Crofts: 17)

Optimum conditions for effective interviewing were described as those in which the interviewer is attentive and sensitive to the person interviewed, attends to non-verbal as well as verbal behaviour, works at achieving a co-operative and harmonious interaction (rapport), avoids responding to outside interruption to create 'psychological privacy' and maintains emotional objectivity.

What has been said so far regarding the behaviour of interviewers can be applied to all manner of clinical interviews and behavioural interviewers have gained by following the principles enunciated earlier. However, a behavioural interview differs from other clinical interviews because of its focus. Behaviour therapists must phrase their questions to gain a clear and unambiguous understanding of the presenting complaints. Ullman and Krasner (1969) suggested 'what' type of questions rather than 'why' questions. Meyer, Liddell and Lyons (1977) added 'how', 'when' and 'where' as queries likely to elicit target behaviour susceptible to change. The influence of Kanfer and Saslow (1965, 1969), who pioneered a strategy for obtaining comprehensive behavioural diagnoses, is acknowledged with special reference to their concern for understanding assets along with the deficits presented by clients. The schema is presented graphically in Fig. 2.1.

Schema for behavioural interviewing

A client usually approaches the consulting room eager and ready to discuss the presenting complaint in some detail. At this stage, the client may or may not share the therapist's behavioural model. If not, interviewer and client need to develop a common language to communicate effectively with each other. A person coming for help is more than a series of complaints, he or she lives in a world of influences outside the clinic and has been subjected to a unique developmental history. The schema presented is designed to obtain a comprehensive personal history including complaints or deficits as well as assets. It is a multi-dimensional approach in which complaints and assets will need to be balanced against each other if effective action is to take place.

Presenting complaints. Making a precise and quantifiable description of the presenting complaint(s) is generally considered the first step to treatment. In any case, the most accessible information usually relates to presenting complaints. Once the client has presented his/her complaint or complaints, the therapist will categorize the description of the problem area as to whether it involves an excess or a deficit behaviour. For instance, excessive responding could be overeating or drinking, heavy smoking or showing uncontrollable anxiety in situations which do not affect most people adversely. On the other hand, examples of deficits are lack of the social skills necessary for functioning comfortably in society or a reduced activity level due to depression. When the complaint is defined, some form of baseline is established for each complaint presented, i.e., how often? how long? how

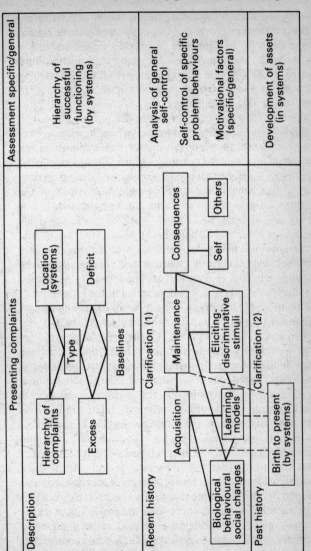

Fig. 2.1 A scheme for behavioural interviews
(Source: Meyer, Liddell and Lyons in *Handbook of Behavioral Assessment*, Wiley, 1977)

severe? To help achieve more precision in the quantification of the problem, one form or other of the specific behavioural assessments (to be discussed later) may be used after the interview has taken place. Each complaint is taken in turn and, if more than one complaint is brought forward, a hierarchy is elicited from the client regarding the order of importance of the complaints.

Making sense of the human behaviour in context is fraught with difficulty. However, while it may appear simpler at first to focus entirely on the client's complaint and current history, it is an expedience which seldoms pays in the long run. A framework drawing from 'general system theory' has been found useful to organize much of the complex information relevant to human functioning. The theory as applied to clinical work was discussed by Sundberg, Tyler and Taplin (1973). Miller (1971) defined a general systems behaviour theory in which there are seven levels of living systems, namely cell, organ, organism, organization, society, and supranational system. As applied to individuals: (1) the cell system refers to the separate cells of the body; (2) the organ system refers to groups of cells organized to make a functional unit such as the nervous system or the digestive system; (3) the organismic system is most closely related to *self*, in other words, it is the individual; (4) the group system refers to such groupings as are closely related to the individual, i.e. family, occupational or recreational groupings; (5) the organizational system refers to large groups of less intimately related individuals than was the case in the previous level, i.e. industrial, professional or social agencies. Levels 6 and 7 extend externally to national and international systems. It is evident from the above that the individual moves within these interrelated systems which vary in terms of location, size and complexity. One of the most appealing characteristics of this theory for the behaviour therapist is the possibility of taking as one's unit of observation a defined set of interacting variables (family, marriage) rather than being confined to single elements. In practice, levels 2, 3, and 4 are the main areas of concern to those who deal with psychological problems – few clients have problems dealing with the United Nations! Problems can sometimes be located in one system only but it is often true that more than one system is affected. In any case, any long-standing problem, however well circumscribed, will have social and interpersonal repercussions which need to be dealt with. The description of the presenting complaint is complete when it has been located as to system. Two areas of clarification supplement the description, one referring to relevant recent history and the other to a chronological development and social past history.

Clarification 1. This is the aspect of behavioural analysis which is most often talked about in the literature. After a problem has been defined operationally (that is, in a manner susceptible to precise quantification), a functional analysis of the client's behaviour and environment is carried out. A widely used model derived from learning theories to identify the relationship between problem behaviour and environment is the ABC model (Cormier & Cormier 1985; Goldiamond 1965; Goodwin 1969; Mahoney & Thoresen 1974; Thoresen & Mahoney 1974). In this model (A) stands for antecedent, that is, an event which cues one on how to behave, (C) are events (consequences) which strengthen or weaken a person's behaviour and (B) is the behaviour under analysis. In the same vein, Goldfried and Sprafkin (1976) presented the acronym SORC for their model; (S) for stimuli or antecedent conditions that make the response better or worse, (O) for organism variables or those physiological variables that may contribute to the problem and its relevant history, (R) is behaviour including motor, physiological-emotional, verbal-cognitive manners of responding, and (C) for short- and long-term consequences maintaining the problem behaviour. The application of the SORC model is discussed by Nelson and Barlow (1981). The influence of learning models is also evident in Clarification (1), in that attempts are made to explain both acquisition and maintenance of each problem presented; eliciting discriminative stimuli and consequences (both to self and others) figure equally in the analysis. Indirectly related events in systems 2, 3, and 4 are also the subjects of the investigation as biological, behavioural and social changes under the assumption that such changes may predispose the individual to resort to maladaptive strategies.

Clarification 2. Details relating to the past history of the individual can be useful in planning a realistic therapeutic programme. With this in view, a chronological developmental, social and occupational history puts the presenting complaint in perspective. The amount and depth of past history information is influenced by the lack of clarity or definition of recent history material. A comprehensive history is more pertinent when the problems presented are pervasive and of long standing, than when they have developed suddenly in a relatively circumscribed area.

Assets. Personality characteristics or dimensions described and measured by personality theorists in the past have been of little use to behaviour therapists, mainly because these characteristics failed to predict therapeutic gains (Mischel 1968). Positive client attributes of interest to therapists are those which centre around self-control and motivation. Clients' assets are also evaluated within each of the operationalizable systems. Specific assets are those directly helpful in dealing with the presenting complaint, while general ones are such features as good coping strategies in general and strong support systems from others.

Case illustration

The schema detailed above is best illustrated by a transcript of a behavioural interview carried out by a psychologist with Mrs A, a 42-year old woman who was referred to a psychology clinic by her GP for agoraphobic symptoms. All identifying details have been changed or eliminated to preserve the client's anonymity.

T: *Can you tell us how you feel agoraphobic or what it is about you that is agoraphobic?*

C: *Well, actually I find everything very hard.*

T: *Like what?*

C: *For instance, going to the supermarket, going to a movie or any department stores.*

T: *What is it that is difficult about that?*

C: *I don't know what actually it is that I'm afraid of, it's just this feeling that gets over me when I get in there.*

T: *Go on.*

C: *I feel as if I am going to pass out. My heart starts pounding. Actually I'm all really uptight over everything.*

T: *Hmm, Hmm.*

C: *I get done what I want to get done as quickly as I can, and the more I'm rushing, the more uptight I'm getting.*

T: *Yes.*

C: *Like when I'm at the checkout, I'm there and the girl seems to be going so slow, checking out my groceries or whatever.*

T: *Yes.*

C: *When I'm there I'm sort of gasping and I feel like saying: Will you please hurry, I've got to get out of here.*

T: *Have you ever actually walked out because it was so awful?*

C: *I have, I've actually had to leave.*

T: *Often?*

C: *Well, I used to stick it out, but it was so hard on me. Now I only go when it is absolutely necessary.*

T: *Does someone else go for you if you can't go?*

C: *Right now no, I've got to go myself because I'm divorced and I've got children and I've got to go to the supermarket and I've got to do shopping.*

T: *So does that mean that you go at least once a week still?*

C: *Oh yes.*

T: *Are there any times when you feel better and you can actually manage without much anxiety?*

C: *Yes, there are times when it's not too bad.*

T: *Do you know what happens during those times, are you more relaxed or is it a different store?*

C: *Well, no, I suffer from severe anxiety anyway and I've been taking medication for the past – gosh – twenty years and I find that if I pop a pill then I can cope pretty well.*

T: *Do you know the names of the medication you take?*

C: *Right now it's (brand name).*

T: *And what did you have before?*

C: *(Brand name) I think.*

T: *Do you know why it was changed to (brand name)?*

C: *Well, I became addicted to (brand name) and they had to take me off.*

T: *So, you have problems going into supermarkets, what other places?*

C: *Church, I find that very, very hard.*

T: *Yes, do you actually still go into your church?*

C: *I go because I feel guilty about not going. The farthest I can go is the outside porch and I sit right down in the back seats.*

T: *Yes.*

C: *I can't get up to the front seats.*

T: *Are there any other situations which are difficult, like going to the bank, for instance? Do you go to the Bank?*

C: *I go but it's just the same as the supermarket.*

T: *So the bank, the supermarket, what about travelling?*

C: *I'm really bound to the home because I don't have any friends because I don't associate, when they ask me to do certain things it's like I'm scared to death when I'm out of my own home.*

T: *Yes, but how did you come here today?*

C: *I got a run in with my daughter and her husband. My daughter makes me feel secure.*

T: *So your daughter is the person who makes you feel secure.
    Does she still take you around?*

C: *Every now and then but I don't like to pressure her too
    much. I've got to stand on my own two feet.*

T: *I'm not sure if this is so, but let's say your daughter hadn't
    got married. Do you think you would have coped and
    wouldn't have wanted any treatment because she was there
    and took you wherever you wanted?*

C: *No, I would have needed treatment because I've been there
    with my daughter.*

T: *So even with your daughter, sometimes it helped but it
    wasn't the only answer.*

C: *Sometimes, the only good of having my daughter with me
    was she had the car so I could get around quickly.*

T: *Yes, so I suppose the main way in which you are travelling
    is when your daughter takes you by car, you wouldn't go
    by bus alone, would you?*

C: *I find it very, very hard on the bus.*

T: *Is it easier for you in a taxi?*

C: *Yes, because you can always say to the cab driver – let me
    out of here.*

T: *Yes, Yes.*

C: *If you want to tell the bus driver, he has got to wait for the
    bus stop.*

T: *Yes, Yes.*

C: *Well, I must say that over the past six years I'm not as scared as I used to be. I can get on the bus. Sometimes it is very hard but I can get on it though.*

T: *How far can you go comfortably away from your home on your own? Could you go and post a letter for instance?*

C: *During the past summer I tried to take a walk every day.*

T: *Oh that was very good.*

C: *For the good of my health you know.*

T: *How far did you go?*

C: *About a half a mile and when I turned around to come home I would panic and I'd say – My God I'm going to die, I'm dying!*

T: *Hmm, Hmm.*

C: *I'm never going to make it, home seemed so far away.*

T: *Yes.*

C: *Then I'd start to run and my heart would be pounding.*

T: *Would the feeling of panic come quickly all of a sudden or would it come gradually – you felt more and more uncomfortable farther from home?*

C: *I guess that was the answer – feeling more uncomfortable, because before I left I would say, I am going to try to go to such a place today and I'd say, well I'm going to get there! Then, I would begin to feel uncomfortable and have to turn back.*

T: *I think that was very clever of you to go out and take a walk like that and try to give yourself goals because what we want to do with you is to help you plan a programme like that. What we're going to do in addition, is give you some skills so that you have some way of controlling your anxiety other than the medication you take and just doing it the way you've done it. But I think it was quite clever of you to do that – did somebody tell you to do it?*

C: *Oh no, I'm very stubborn but sometimes I get discouraged and it takes so much out of me.*

T: *You described how it felt to feel like that – you were talking about your heart racing, what else?*

C: *My mouth gets dry and actually I'm not breathing properly. It is a terrible feeling.*

T: *Those are all the signs of extreme anxiety. If for instance, you had a lion chasing you, you'd feel just like that. Unfortunately it is happening in situations which are not that dangerous. You said you have been on medication for something like twenty years, so would you say that that problem had been around for twenty years?*

C: *I've had this for, I guess, just as far back as I can remember. I was only about twelve years old and that's when I can remember becoming really scared and frightened.*

T: *Do you remember if anything happened to scare you at the time?*

C: *Well, I was always a very nervous, frightened child, frightening things that happened when I was a child make me like that. I know that now.*

T: *What did you think they were?*

C: *For instance, my mother died when I was a baby and my aunt looked after me. I didn't know my father, he had gone off and married someone else. I can remember being always scared and clinging to my aunt. And then, at seven, I was taken away from her by my father whom I didn't know. I was told my aunt could no longer look after me.*

T: *Yes.*

C: *I remember Dad coming to get me, he was a total stranger.*

T: *You hadn't seen him before.*

C: *Not that I could remember.*

T: *Yes.*

C: *And I was awfully afraid to be with him.*

T: *I'm sure it was very frightening. So you moved with your father when you were seven.*

C: *Yes, I was supposed to live with him but when I got up to the place where I was supposed to live in – I cried to go with my grandmother, so my grandmother took me.*

T: *Hmm, Hmm.*

C: *I was scared of her.*

T: *Yes.*

C. *She was a very strict lady to live with and she barred me up, she wouldn't let me go out with the other girls because they were going to be bad examples for me. Some evenings she'd send me to bed early with my prayer book.*

T: *So she was very religious?*

C: *Church was very important to her. I was scared – I was scared of everything.*

T: *Was there a grandfather too?*

C: *Yes.*

T: *Was he less strict?*

C: *Yes, he was a dear old man. He was afraid of her too.*

T: *So you chose to live with your grandmother but perhaps it would have been better to live with your father.*

C: *No, I don't think so because my stepmother didn't like me. My grandmother loved me as much as she could, she did what she thought was best for me. All in all my childhood was full of scary things.*

T: *So, from the age of seven, you lived with your grandmother and she was strict and isolated you from other people expecting very high moral standards. I suppose that sometimes you must have thought how long is that going to last since you had been moved before without your consent. Did you feel that perhaps she would die and you would have to go to your father? What sort of thoughts did you have?*

C: *I never thought that. I often thought of running away somewhere – and even jumping over a wharf.*

T: *So you weren't a very happy child?*

C: *No, I was very unhappy and very scared and worried about everything.*

T: *What sort of things did you worry about?*

C: *Well, I remember one day in particular I worried when I started menstruating she said – Oh dear, you're not going over there anymore – and I didn't know why because I couldn't help it. Of course when I started menstruating I didn't know what was wrong with me – they didn't come right out and tell me, so I went to an aunt and she sent me off to another. Anyway the next aunt said – if a boy touches you you'll have a baby.*

T: *Hmm, Hmm.*

C: *That's the way she explained it. So, in school, there used to be this boy who used to sit behind me and he had a habit of, every chance he'd get, he'd hold my hand. I went around with this inside me for so long – he'd touched me so I'm having a baby. I actually used to come home from school and hear a baby crying inside of me, and I couldn't tell anyone.*

T: *Did you make some friends at school?*

C: *Well yes, I had friends but I couldn't go out with them on picnics or anything.*

T: *Did you like school though, the school work, were you a good scholar?*

C: *I was pretty good but I came to this stage at twelve or thirteen though when I got this problem. Whatever happened to me then I just don't know. I think, it was a nervous breakdown.*

T: *How would you describe this breakdown? Did you get more afraid?*

C: *Yes, I can remember before that, I could do things and not be scared.*

T: *Hmm. Hmm.*

C: *At this age, it would come to me all of a sudden and I'd just run out of school and run right home gasping for breath.*

T: *So you must have missed quite a lot of school?*

C: *I did, for a year or so, I missed quite a lot.*

T: *How did people react to you then – did they send you to get some treatment?*

C: *No, my grandmother used to take me to the priest and he would bless me and my heart was pounding the whole time.*

T: *Did you think, then, that you had a heart condition?*

C: *Oh yes, I was sure of it and I probably still am. I would dwell on my heart and I'd be feeling my pulse. That was the one thing on my mind.*

T: *Yes, so that must have been very frightening. The moment you got anxious you felt that you were damaging yourself as well as being anxious.*

C: *That's right.*

T: *And you say it lasted for a year, then what happened?*

C: *Yes, for about a year, I went down and lost a lot of weight. Then I got back in school and I don't know how I felt, but I got back in school but school wasn't school, it was harder for me then.*

T: *You must have missed quite a lot of teaching.*

C: *So at sixteen, I met my ex-husband.*

T: *Was he at school with you?*

C: *No.*

T: *How did you meet him?*

C: *Well, he did belong to the same area.*

T: *Hmm, Hmm.*

C: *And, actually I saw him at a dance – my grandmother was sitting by me but I was able to sneak a dance.*

T: *Yes.*

C: *So, at sixteen anyway, I don't know how, but she let me go out for a drive with him – right now, I wish she hadn't.*

T: *Yes, but at the time, he was your first boyfriend.*

C: *Oh yes, I was really in love.*

T: *Was he older than you?*

C: *Three years older than me.*

T: *Yes, so he was nineteen and he was working, I suppose.*

C: *Yes.*

T: *What was special about him other than the first one?*

C: *Oh, I don't know, he was handsome and there was so much love in me. He was so polite.*

T: *Yes.*

C: *So, she tried to break me up with him after a while, she thought I was seeing him too much – then, I went downhill again.*

T: *How did she succeed because by then you were sixteen years of age?*

C: *Yes, well like I say, I was on a hunger strike. My grandmother said if we don't let her marry she will die anyway so she consented.*

T: *Does that mean you needed to be ill to have someone listen to you? Could you not say – look, I'm old enough, I want such and such. Could you not speak back to her?*

C: *No, I never spoke back to my grandmother.*

T: *So, it was the only way out?*

C: *Well, come to think about this now, maybe that was my way. I don't know – well no, I didn't want to be that way.*

T: *So you married at seventeen.*

C: *Yes.*

T: *Was that ever happy?*

C: *Oh my, I thought that the other years were hell but this was worse. He was an alcoholic.*

T: *Did you know that, when you married him?*

C: *No, well, I knew he drank a bit.*

T: *What was his job?*

C: *He was just an assistant school caretaker and he got other jobs after that.*

T: *Yes, was it through his alcoholism that he had to change?*

C: *Yes, and I got pregnant one after the other, you know.*

T: *Yes, how many children have you?*

C: *I have five children, but had six.*

T: *Hmm.*

C: *It became so bad that I was living in fear for my life. He tried to choke me – he put his hands around my throat.*

T: *Hmm.*

C: *Like I say, it was hell.*

T: *How long did you have with him?*

C: *Twenty years.*

T: *Goodness, so you must have had a very unhappy time.*

C: *Yes, I had a few nervous breakdowns and was in St Elsewhere's Psychiatric ward and I had to take medication.*

T: *When you had those breakdowns, what was it like mainly, being depressed, anxious or what?*

C: *Anxious, mostly.*

T: *Hmm, Hmm.*

C: *It's hard to describe it – I'd be depressed and I couldn't stand it.*

T: *When was the first time you went to St Elsewhere?*

C: *It was after my boy died – three weeks after that – it was
     on Christmas Eve morning.*

T: *Oh, dear, how distressing.*

C: *He was born in (date) and died when he was almost three
     years.*

T: *Was he ill?*

C: *No, he died very suddenly – he was just perfect the day
     before you know, going around and everything.*

T: *That must have been a terrible shock.*

C: *It was – I was five months pregnant at the time.*

T: *Was he your first child?*

C: *No, he was my second.*

T: *And, do you know why he died?*

C: *They said he haemorrhaged in his lungs.*

T: *And, you had no way of knowing.*

C: *That night he had a fever, coughing and gasping. Seven
     o'clock in the morning. I asked him how he was and he
     said, I'm better. He was smiling and, a couple of minutes
     after that, I turned and went out and I heard a choking
     sound, I turned around and he just died.*

T: *Was your husband around then?*

C: *He was there in the morning but he was out drinking in the
     night. He was there when he died because he took him up in
     his arms. A few years after, while he'd be drunk, he'd come*

in and say in front of the other people and our children –
You murdered our son!

T: *He would do that just when he was drunk? So he was very*
distressed about that himself?

C: *He must have been I thought, to say something like that to*
me. I couldn't understand it and my other children there
you know and they'd probably believe him because, well, I
was their mother and, well, he was their father.

T: *Did you blame yourself as well?*

C: *Not really because I know the way things are because I*
couldn't hold myself responsible but sometimes I did.

T: *Yes.*

C: *I was waiting up till daylight. I really didn't know he was*
that sick.

T: *Yes, it's very difficult with small children because most of*
the time they do get better. That's the time when you went
to St Elsewhere's just after that?

C: *Yes, just after that.*

T: *Was that the first time after you were married?*

C: *Yes.*

T: *Did they take you as an in-patient?*

C: *Yes.*

T: *Do you remember how long you spent?*

C: *I think I was there about three weeks.*

T: *Who looked after your children while you were away?*

C: *He put them in a home, after I went to the hospital.*

T: *That must have been rather difficult for you.*

C: *It was really hard and I prayed to God that I would get back to them because, as far as I was concerned, he shouldn't have put them in there.*

T: *Was he good to the children, did he hit them?*

C: *He never did touch our children.*

T: *Did he hit you?*

C: *Me, yes, like I said he would grab me by the throat.*

T: *So that must have been a very frightening time.*

C: *It was a very frightening time, it was very frightening for my children.*

T: *Would they take your side, do you think?*

C: *All the time.*

T: *Is the daughter who takes you around the oldest in the family?*

C: *Yes, she is.*

T: *How old is she now?*

C: *Twenty-two years. She is a registered nurse.*

T: *What about the next one?*

C: *He is twenty.*

T: *Twenty, and what does he do?*

C: *He is in (town) with his father.*

T: *So he went with his father, was that his choice?*

C: *Yes, he had just finished school and his father suggested he go out and get a job with him in (town).*

T: *What is your ex-husband doing in (town)?*

C: *I think carpenter work but I'm not sure.*

T: *What about the next child?*

C: *Susie, she's nineteen years and she is married.*

T: *How long has she been married?*

C: *Since August, the August past she got married.*

T: *Yes, so you've lost your two daughters.*

C: *Yes, my two daughters and a son.*

T: *And the next one?*

C: *That's Jenny, she's seventeen years.*

T: *Is she still at home?*

C: *Yes, she is in grade 12 and Tom, he is fourteen years.*

T: *I suppose he is at school too. At any rate do you think your children have made up for your bad marriage?*

C: *They're just great. They're always confident – well, one, she turned against him, she was sort of a bit close to her father but I don't know, I don't think she should feel that way, he is an alcoholic and its not his fault but its up to herself.*

T: *When your two elder daughters married, it must have made quite a void in your life.*

C: *Yes, it has, especially the last one, I guess I depended on her.*

T: *Now, how do you think you're going to manage without them?*

C: *I am coping pretty well. I got over it quickly. I was depressed for a while but now I feel better.*

T: *So you went to St Elsewhere's for the first time after the death of your son and when was the next time you went to St Elsewhere's?*

C: *I really can't remember the exact dates or anything like that. I probably used to get three or four years out of it.*

T: *Yes, so every three or four years. Would something happen or was it enough to have to cope with your marriage?*

C: *Yes, everything built up, I'd get sick and I'd be awake all night.*

T: *Yes.*

C: *And being home had been so bad – he'd break the place up, I'd take the young ones and go somewhere and I'd have to go back to the same situation.*

T: *Of course it wasn't easy for you not having a family, where would you go?*

C: *I didn't have anywhere to go and none of my family knew what I was going through because I didn't tell them because I felt, what's the point, I can't go back to them now.*

T: *What made you stay so long? Twenty years is a long time. You've been very loyal.*

C: *Because I was scared of him.*

T: *Did you also dread the move and doing something on your own if you left?*

C: *I was afraid he would take the children. You know he had me down to such a low level, I had no self-confidence. I never had much anyway but the bit I had, I had lost.*

T: *And, what made you decide to end your marriage?*

C: *Actually he made it sort of easy for me. The last going off, he was having an affair with a girl a little older than my oldest daughter and I don't know what came over me, I just sort of, I got really mad and got the separation which didn't cause very much pain.*

T: *Yes, because you put up with it for so long. Did you feel pleased that you had finally done something about it?*

C: *I was really, really proud of myself because he said I'm going to (town) and he said that after a few months we could probably get back together providing, he said, I kept my nose clean, that I didn't go around with anyone else. He went to (town) and he sent me some money and he was calling often telling me how much he loved me and anyway*

I ended up taking him back again. I hated myself for doing that but he came back again.

T: *How long ago was that?*

C: *That was about four years ago.*

T: *Yes, how long did that last?*

C: *That lasted for about four or five months.*

T: *Was he any good then?*

C: *He tried very hard, but I found I had no faith in him whatsoever.*

T: *Did he ever try to get help with his drinking?*

C: *At one time, when I left home and he thought I was really going to stay away, he came and begged me to go back and that he'd go to AA.*

T: *Yes.*

C: *So I went back and he went to AA a few times.*

T: *Hmm, Hmm.*

C: *But he'd come home and he'd call them a crowd of fools and this sort of thing.*

T: *Yes.*

C: *I think around Christmas time he went to a club again and he came back at Christmas and he ended up knocking the Christmas tree across the house and everyone was scared and it was the merry-go-round all over again.*

T: *Yes, you had seen it all before.*

C: *My oldest girl turned around and she said – Mom get rid of him. That's what I wanted to hear. So I told him, I was getting a divorce and he went back to his other friends in (town) and I was frightened to death. So thank God, I'm divorced now.*

T: *When was that?*

C: *It will be three years.*

T: *And, has he bothered you at all since then?*

C: *He phones every now and then from (town) when he is drunk. I'm glad he is in (town) because even though we're divorced, I'd still be scared if he was around here.*

T: *Yes, of course. What has happened to you in the last three years – has your life improved?*

C: *It has because, thank God, the conditions I was living under for the past twenty years weren't very good. I've gotten a nice place to live, I'm comfortable and warm.*

T: *Are you working at all?*

C: *People ask me that so often. How can I work when I'm scared to death to be out there. I'd love to be, even if it was a part-time job.*

T: *You haven't worked at all since you've been married, in fact you haven't worked ever, have you?*

C: *I took on a part-time job some years ago and it was just a grocery store. It was really bad, you know I was really terrified.*

T: *Yes, so it wasn't really nice. Have you found a new boyfriend?*

C: *I joined a group, it's called (name), have you heard of it?*

T: *No, I don't know about this one.*

C: *It is the Association of Separated and Divorced.*

T: *Yes.*

C: *I went to see what that was all about because it was quite new to me, you know. I did date a couple of men, like at house parties and things like that, but I find I'm really not that interested in anything serious. I don't know if I could handle it again.*

T: *Well, you have had a very bad experience haven't you?*

C: *That's true.*

T: *How do you manage for money?*

C: *(Husband) supported me for a long while but now I find it very hard to be on social assistance.*

C: *Yes, but I was surprised to hear that you were warmer and had a better house.*

C: *Well, they're OK – it's all subsidized housing from (council).*

T: *Really now your life is more quiet, you're not threatened by anything really and you are more comfortable than you have ever been. Would you say that if you didn't have these symptoms, not being able to get out, life would be almost 100 per cent right for you?*

C: *Oh yes, it would because I could go and get some kind of a new job. My children aren't home now so I don't have to worry and when they do come home, they can sort of get themselves something, but I'm in a trap whichever way I turn.*

T: *When did people decide that you had enough of (brand name) medication? Was it because you kept going in and out of St Elsewhere's.*

C: *Yes.*

T: *And, who was looking after you there?*

C: *Dr X*

T: *Is he still looking after you?*

C: *No, he's not very good – Dr XX is looking after me now.*

T: *So you're still seeing him.*

C: *Yes, I see him once a month and he gives me a prescription.*

T: *What does he say has been wrong with you?*

C: *Well, Dr XX I'm not sure – he doesn't talk to me very much. I don't even believe he knows about this agoraphobia.*

T: *What has he treated you for?*

C: *He knows about my heartbeats.*

T: *So you just go to get the medication.*

C: *That's it.*

T: *And how did your GP get involved? He sounded very concerned about you.*

C: *Dr XXX is my family doctor.*

T: *Has he been your family doctor for a very long time?*

C: *No, only for about the past six months. I changed doctors and went to him.*

T: *Why did you change?*

C: *I wanted a change. I lost a bit of faith. I went to Dr XXX and I don't know how this came about but he is just so nice and comfortable to talk to that, one day, it sort of came out and he really took an interest in it. Everytime I'd go in he talked to me and told me he was going to try and get me some help and, you know, I really appreciated it.*

T: *What has your medical history been like? Have you had a lot of medical problems because I see that you visit your GP quite a lot.*

C: *I had meningitis, I had a hysterectomy.*

T: *When did you have meningitis, that's a bit of a knock isn't it?*

C: *I had meningitis, I'd say, about twelve years ago.*

T: *Yes, that must have been rather difficult to cope with the family and everything.*

C: *Yes, because it was bad, I was in hospital for lots of other things besides that.*

T: *So the meningitis twelve years ago.*

C: *Yes, the hysterectomy.*

T: *When was that, recently?*

C: *That was about eleven years ago.*

T: *What was the problem, do you know?*

C: *No, I don't know. I still got my ovaries. They didn't give me any real reason for it. I don't know, they didn't tell me if it was cancer or anything like that.*

T: *Did you ask them?*

C: *No, I didn't ask anything, I guess I was afraid to ask.*

T: *What else has been bothering you? What else have you been treated for?*

C: *I had my appendix out, I had surgery on an ovarian cyst last summer.*

T: *So your health hasn't been that good, has it?*

C: *No.*

T: *Were you a sickly child?*

C: *No, I don't remember being sick as a child.*

T: *And, do you feel now that your health is pretty good?*

C: *Well sometimes I don't know – sometimes I feel pretty miserable. I still have pains like I had before they removed my cyst.*

T: *I know you've been worrying about your heart – have you ever asked your GP for an investigation into that?*

C: *Oh yes, I've asked.*

T: *So how often have they investigated you for your heart?*

C: *Each time I was in the hospital and I went to a heart specialist.*

T: *You've had a combination of worries about your health but then, sometimes, you had some pretty good reasons to get worried.*

C: *Yes, because there is often something there.*

T: *Other than your heart, have you worried about other things? Have you got other investigations.*

C: *Well right now, I'm worried about this pain and cancer and things like that.*

T: *Yes, what has Dr XXX told you about it?*

C: *That, if it doesn't go, he'll send me back to the hospital but I don't really want to go back.*

T: *So you don't like hospitals either?*

C: *Oh no, I've been in there so many times but, right now, I want everything to go so good I don't want to go in there anymore.*

T: *Yes, so is that why you changed your GP, because you didn't believe what he was telling you or you thought he wasn't giving you enough attention?*

C: *Well, actually I was going to switch doctors before but I got this pain in my side and you know he was treating me for a kidney infection, a bladder infection and everything except the ovarian cyst.*

T: *Did you have infections quite often as well?*

C: *Oh yes, and then I went to Dr XXX one time and he said something about a cyst and checked me out and put me in the hospital. Dr XXX treated me well and he knows, if there is anything worrying me, and he has checked me out where other doctors wouldn't have. I have all the faith in the world in him.*

T: *So you feel you're in good hands.*

C: *I do.*

T: *How worried are you about your health now?*

C: *I am worried because I don't feel well lately – I also have a back pain. I worry about it then I say, what the heck if I have cancer, I go and I'm still here.*

T: *But it is still worrying to think that you may have it.*

C: *Yes, it is.*

T: *Do you have good moments when you think, well perhaps I'm being a little bit illogical about this.*

C: *I guess sometimes that I get fed up. I really say the pain is there and if it is cancer it can stay. I don't want to go to the doctor and end up in the hospital and I'm sick of it all, you know.*

T: *Several things over all these years like your marriage, your health and going in and out of hospital have made your life a little bit different from other people.*

C: *Yes, very much different.*

T: *Well, I think you've been very patient. You've given me a lot of helpful details – I'll tell you about the programme that we have here. What we want to do is to work out a way to help you control your fears. I think you've been very courageous going out when you were afraid and it's very much the same sort of thing that we want to do with you. One common problem is that people like you either push it too much or too little so we want to teach you a realistic way of exposing yourself to what you have avoided. It will be things like that. We're going to ask you to think of situations which you avoid, situations which you could practise on your own, like going for a walk, like going to the supermarket, etc. and work out every week something for you to do. If it is not working out, we'll find something else, something less frightening. The programme is five weeks because at the same time we think of anxiety as having three different aspects, there may be other parts but at the moment we can identify three. One of them is that you avoid these situations, when you're anxious you don't go, you stop going and the more you stop going, the more you run away from it, the more anxious you are because, in the long run, you become afraid of your own fear feelings. Well, we all know that and, it is easier said than done, to say that. What you need to do is go back and do it. There are things that we can teach you to do to help. Your body responds doesn't it? You've talked about a dry throat and you've talked about shaking and that sort of thing. So one of the skills we're going to teach you is to relax your body and I wondered if you had done something like that at St Elsewhere's?*

C: *No.*

T: *What we're going to do as part of the programme, is to give you physical relaxation training and ask you to practise on your own, so that you gradually get more relaxed, more control over the bodily signs of your anxiety. The other aspect of anxiety is what you're* thinking when you are afraid. Well honestly, with your history, it's difficult to think of what is left to happen which can be bad. You worry a lot but I'm not surprised because a lot of things happened to teach you to worry but, sometimes, you worry unnecessarily about your health. I'm not surprised that you've learned to worry and anticipate the worst and it has happened to you sometimes. What I'm trying to say is that there is a part which is thinking of anxiety and worrying and it makes it worse. Now, if I say to you I'd like you to go to the supermarket now, what would you think, what would you say to yourself?

C: *Right now?*

T: *Yes.*

C: *I'd say, I'd give it a try.*

T: *I think you're very good there – it's not quite what I was expecting you to say. You seem to be very determined but what I was trying to show is that some people would say to themselves, perhaps I can't do it or I can't stand it, etc. What you think before you avoid something also makes you anxious. You tend to have a lot of negative feelings about your health. If you say to yourself, I think I'm going to have a heart attack, well that's enough to paralyse anybody, isn't it? So what we want is to change people's negative way of thinking. You've given good alternatives already like, perhaps I haven't got it if I'm still around, it can't be that bad and all that sort of thing. So, we're going to teach you to change or alter negative ways of thinking which make you more afraid and gradually over the weeks we're going to teach you to work out a programme. After five weeks we're going to ask you to carry on yourself because you're going to become your own therapist and work out your own programme. By then you'll have the information we've given you about the programme, about relaxing, about changing your thoughts, about planning a realistic programme and we'll ask you to carry on by yourself for another five weeks and then come back to tell us how it went. Usually after those ten weeks, people can manage to do quite a bit on their own but the secret is to be as determined as you are about trying. This does require you to come for five weeks in a row. Does that make any sense to you?*

C: *Yes it does, I was thinking how are we going to do it all?*

T: *Oh, we're going to do it one step at a time and think of it as a learning experience in which you learn to monitor yourself to understand yourself and to become your own therapist. Because of this, we're going to give you a lot of things to take home like forms to fill, your own description of the problem so that you can understand everything better as the programme progresses.*

C: *Right.*

T: *We'd like to do it, as a group, because I think the group members help each other in the sense that they share how they manage to do things and also very often people feel quite isolated. I don't think this is the case with you because you've been to St Elsewhere and you know there are other people feeling exactly as you do and some people feel even worse. A lot of people have not had any treatment and feel that they are the only people in the world, so seeing other people struggle doing the same thing helps many people. Do you want to ask anything about that?*

C: *The part I'm interested in now is what you said about bodily control. Will I remember, when I become panicky?*

T: *That's why we want to do little steps at a time so that it becomes more and more automatic for you to remember what to do, when you have the big things to confront.*

C: *When I get a panic attack I think that, the next time, I won't let it get to me but it still gets to me.*

T: *I understand. What we want to plan is that you experience, and engineer something you can cope with that does bring anxiety, but not too much and learn to control yourself. Then the anxiety subsides and you can see it go down and then you care less. It will be getting more and more automatic and you won't let it rise quite as much as you did before. Certainly, all of us will have crises because anxiety is a normal reaction – if you did not feel any anxiety you would probably not survive childhood because that's why, for example, we don't cross the street without looking. That's why, we avoid going into dangerous and harmful situations. Being anxious is normal and it is also adaptive. You need it to keep you out of danger, but you show too much of it. You've got an excess – you're afraid of too many things, but we don't want you to stop being anxious because that is your own natural protection. We want you to be anxious for reasons that are truly dangerous.*

During the interview, the therapist encouraged Mrs A to present her own description of her problems and judicious questioning steered her towards a behavioural formulation of those problems. Relevant background information relating to onset, previous treatment along with an extensive social and personal history were elicited. The therapist, in turn, shared her own understanding of the client's problems. The interview ended with the therapist presenting the broad outline of a group programme for agoraphobic clients. Details of this programme and Mrs A's response to it will be taken up in subsequent chapters to illustrate characteristic methods of changing behaviour and the principles of evaluating treatment changes.

Specific behavioural assessment techniques

Psychometrics is an area of psychology which aims to

measure specific aspects of human performance. Some of the early assumptions made by the psychologists involved related to the belief that all people possess the same psychological characteristics or traits but in different amounts. While the assumption regarding stability of human traits has been invalidated by such reviews as that of Mischel (1968), the psychometric approach to testing has nevertheless been responsible for the establishment of criteria to evaluate instruments purporting to measure the many facets of human nature. It is therefore commonly accepted that assessment procedures must demonstrate their *reliability* and *validity*. Reliability in the psychometric sense refers to the use of statistical techniques to show that a measure is capable of yielding the same result, if repeated a second time, and validity, that the same instrument measures what it claims to measure. A number of authors have dealt with the psychometric issues relating to behavioural assessment (Cone 1981; Goldfried & Linehan 1977; Haynes 1978; Kendall 1984; Livingston 1977; Nelson 1983).

Ciminero (1977) compared traditional methods with behavioural ones. One of the main drawbacks attributed to traditional assessment techniques was that they tended to be indirectly rather than directly related to treatment. For instance, the Rorschach Test, an elaborate form of ink-blot test needing a great deal of interpretation, has shown little validity for the therapist, as have various forms of symptom/sign inventories. Broadly speaking, behavioural assessments can be classified under three general headings, according to the manner in which the information is obtained. Thus, behaviour therapists gather their information by self-report from clients, by direct observation or by mechanically monitoring a particular physiological function. These were subdivided by Cone and Hawkins (1977) into interviews, self-reports, rating by others, self-observation, direct observation and by Haynes (1978) into naturalistic observation, structured situation assessment, interviews, questionnaires, self-monitoring and psychophysiological assessment. Kendall (1984) stated that 'Assessments of behavior, physiology, and cognition are the hallmark of comprehensive measurement' (Kendall 1984: 64). This is generally operationalized into assessment of the following three response systems: the overt-motor, the physiological-emotional and the verbal-cognitive. The importance of carrying out comprehensive measurement stems from the fact that the three modes of responding so far identified have shown not to co-vary together under certain treatment conditions in studies of animals and humans (Hodgson & Rachman 1974; Mineka 1979; Rachman & Hodgson 1974; Schroeder & Rich 1976).

Self-report

The least structured method of self-report is probably the behavioural interview. However, as was shown in the case report above, the behavioural interview needs to be a planned and guided enterprise to achieve its purpose. The interview should as much as possible tap the three response systems. Other methods of collecting self-reports are through written surveys and inventories. Examples of these include inventories to evaluate fearful behaviour, assertion, depression, sexual orientation and other characteristic problem behaviour brought for attention. Details of the various self-report assessments can be found in the hand-books of behavioural assessments listed at the beginning of the chapter. In the same vein, clients can be required to monitor their own behaviour outside the clinic. Of all the behavioural methods of assessment, surveys and inventories have been designed most closely to comply with psychometric principles. Other methods have encountered problems needing to be tackled in different ways. For instance, self-monitoring is susceptible not only to unreliability but also to reactivity. Reactivity is a well documented phenomenon which makes the very act of self-monitoring cause the behaviour to change in frequency. Desirable behaviour is often seen to increase in frequency and undesirable behaviour generally decreases.

Although all three modes of responding can be collected

by self-report techniques, they have more often been used in the past to assess the verbal-cognitive response system than the other two. A notable exception is the Symptom Questionnaire designed by Lehrer and Woolfolk (1982) as a self-report measure to assess experienced anxiety in somatic, cognitive and behavioural modalities. The authors have conducted a series of validation studies to support its psychometric properties. Another technique which can be adapted to the three response modalities is *Discan*, a scaling method based on sequential paired comparisons of individually phrased reference levels. The method offers better precision in evaluating subjective variables than the traditional rating scales as well as demonstrable reliability (Singh & Bilsbury 1982, 1984a, 1984b).

Direct behavioural observation

Observation carried out by an independent observer has been the essence of behavioural assessment. Such direct behavioural assessment can be carried out on the client's homegrounds. For instance, a behaviour therapist may go to a supermarket with an agoraphobic client to record how long the client actually stays in the feared situation and examine which aspects of the situation are most strongly avoided by the client. It is only fair to add that the resultant observations are not free from distortion. Reactivity and observer bias need to be taken into account when asking an observer for ratings of another person.

Physiological monitoring

A new technology based on a wide range of sophisticated and often costly equipment has developed to monitor various physiological responses. For example, tension can be assessed and relaxation improved by means of information feedback which is presented as a tone or visual signal determined by the level of muscle tension monitored on equipment adapted to reflect the electromyographic (EMG) activity of various muscle groups.

It should be obvious to the reader at this point that behavioural assessment techniques are numerous and varied and the assessment should be carried out at the level of the individual as well as be intimately related to the functional analysis of the problem to be treated.

Chapter 3

Changing overt responses

Psychologically based intervention procedures were initially developed for the treatment of psychiatric disorders – particularly the neuroses and the psychoses. However, neurotic disorders generally proved more responsive to psychological therapies than psychoses. While the application of behaviour therapy is no longer limited to the so-called neurotic problems, it is nevertheless with these kinds of problems that the first behaviour therapists tested their methods. In an evaluation of behaviour therapy with adult neurosis Marks (1978) gave it *a vital part in the management of selected neurosis in the narrower sense.* In addition to phobic and obsessive-compulsive disorders, his review included such conditions as neurotic depression, sexual dysfunction, sexual deviation, stammering, tics and spasms. Marks concluded that behaviour therapy is the treatment of choice in several well-defined neurotic syndromes amounting to 10 per cent of all psychiatric outpatients. However, it is well known that psychiatrists are not consulted for all acknowledged psychological problems. For instance, from a survey of GPs practising in a densely populated Health District of London, it was found that GPs estimated a substantial proportion of their patients to have psychological problems which they treated themselves (Liddell, May, Boyle & Baker 1981). While they sent many of the patients they did not treat directly to psychiatrists, they also referred patients with psychological problems to social workers and marriage guidance counsellors, among others. In recent years, clinical psychologists have increased their contribution to the behavioural treatment of psychological problems outside departments of psychiatry, strengthening their links with other aspects of medicine (Liddell 1983b; McPherson & Sutton 1981).

The types of psychological problem brought to the attention of mental health providers, as well as to others not exclusively involved with them, has changed over the years. Individuals are coming forward with problems which do not fit into the strict criteria for neurotic or psychotic illness. Many clients, for instance, present with problematic but transient states of emotional disturbances. ICD-9 reflected this diversity by instituting categories of adjustment and stress reactions. Under this system, a diagnosis of acute reaction to stress is applicable to a transient state precipitated by unusually severe mental or physical stressors. Adjustment reaction, on the other hand, is reserved for use when the reaction is more prolonged, usually in response to stress of a less spectacular nature and of a longer duration. Recognition of stress reactions is also possible under DSM-III, which is a broader classification system than DSM-II was, by virtue of its multi-axial scheme. Axis I, for instance, can accommodate such conditions as uncomplicated bereavement or parent-child problems and the nature of the psychosocial stressor is identified and evaluated under Axis IV.

Medicine has also felt the need to reappraise some of its basic assumptions. Several influences converged to make a biopsychosocial approach to the understanding and treatment of various diseases appealing. Not least of these influences is the development and acceptance of the behavioural sciences and their inclusion in the syllabuses of medical schools. A new field of behavioural medicine emerged in the mid-1970s spurred by the success of behaviour therapy and applied behaviour analysis. What is thought to be the first published definition of behavioural medicine was coined by Schwartz and Weiss (1977) and ran thus:

Behavioral medicine is the field concerned with the development of behavioral science knowledge and techniques relevant to the understanding of physical health and illness and the application of this knowledge and these techniques to diagnosis, prevention, treatment and rehabilitation. Psychosis, neurosis and substance abuse are included only insofar as they contribute to physical disorders as an end point (Schwartz & Weiss 1977 Proceedings of the Yale conference on behavioral medicine, US Government Printing Office: 379).

Pomerlau and Brady (1979) emphasized the role of modern behaviourism and that of experimental behavioural sciences in another contemporary definition:

Behavioral medicine can be defined as (a) the clinical use of techniques derived from the experimental analysis of behavior – behavior therapy and behavior modification – for the evaluation, prevention, management, or treatment of physical disease or physiological dysfunction; and (b) the conduct of research contributing to the functional analysis and understanding of behavior associated with medical disorders and problems in health care (Pomerleau & Brady 1979, *Behavioral Medicine: Theory and Practice*, Williams and Wilkins: xxi).

In the foreword to a book entitled *Behavioral Medicine: Practical Applications in Health Care*, Lang (1980) raised the possibility that behaviour therapy may be more effective in general medicine than it has been in psychiatry.

In sum, many psychological problems are seen outside psychiatry and treated by a variety of suitably trained professionals other than psychiatrists. Stress hypotheses have gained momentum in recent years, making possible the identification of groups at risk and the establishment of preventive work. Bellack, Hersen and Kazdin (1982) edited an *International Handbook of Behavior Modification and Therapy* from which it is possible to assess the efficacy of such varied interventions as increasing pleasant activities and decreasing unpleasant ones in depression, relaxation techniques and/or biofeedback to reduce blood pressure levels, various multimodal approaches to the elimination of addictive behaviour relating to drugs, eating and smoking, skills training for sexual and interpersonal problems and methods to enhance compliance to various treatment regimens. Krasner (1985) baulked at the task of reviewing the book, stating that it was more in the nature of an encyclopaedia than a handbook!

Procedures to change overt behaviour

The most important guideline in the choice of problems to be targeted for change is that the problem behaviour be operationalizable. In other words, what a person *does* in certain situations. This procedure enables both client and therapist to observe and quantify each problem reliably. Initially, behaviour therapists encouraged their clients to choose visible behaviour in preference to covert or invisible events. Using the terminology drawn from the psychology of learning, Goldfried (1982) stressed the importance of differentiating responses that are primarily *respondents* from those that are *operants*. In his words:

Respondents, where consequences play a relatively minimal role in maintaining the response, typically include such emotional reactions as anxiety, depression, anger and sexual arousal. Operant or instrumental behavior, on the other hand, includes those responses for which the consequent reinforcement plays a significant role. Examples of maladaptive instrumental behavior are typically seen in children, particularly where the primary difficulty consists of 'behavior problems'. The extensive work done with token economies in schools and institutional settings has similarly focused on instrumental behaviors. Still further examples of operant behavior seen in clinical settings are social skill deficits, such as lack of assertiveness and inappropriate heterosexual behaviors (Goldfried 1982, Behavioral assessment, in Bellack, M. *et al. Handbook of Behavior Modification and Therapy*, Plenum: 99).

He cautioned that there are times when the distinction between respondents and operants is not clear-cut. An example of behaviour difficult to classify would be the case of a client who avoids going into supermarkets for fear of panicking and whose family and friends take turns in doing her shopping. For a description of the learning principles relevant to behaviour therapy, the reader is referred to Levis (1982) or Wilson and O'Leary (1980).

Changing respondents

Wolpe's (1958) *Psychotherapy by Reciprocal Inhibition* crystallized the behaviourists' aspirations to alleviate human suffering in the clinic using the principles of experimental psychology. Wolpe's approach comprised all the main elements which were to become the belief system of behaviour therapists, that is, the formulation of testable concepts, research based on the learning paradigm and the integration of data ranging from simple animal behaviour to the complexity of behaviour brought by clients into the clinic. Systematic desensitization was offered and taken up widely as an explicit strategy for behaviour change making research and treatment inseparable. Systematic desensitization was aimed primarily at changing maladaptive anxiety. Before describing and justifying the procedure, it is necessary to place anxiety based disorders in perspective as to their contribution to human suffering. Freedman, Dornbush and Shapiro (1981), a group of representative American psychiatrists, stated: 'Anxiety is the most common psychopathologic symptom that is manifest in mental illness, as well as in everyday life. Anxiety is present in the mildest to the most severe emotional disturbances, from transient states to major psychosis' (Freedman *et al*. 1981, Anxiety: Here today and here tomorrow, *Comprehensive Psychiatry*: 44).

Systematic desensitization based on relaxation. Wolpe's therapy was derived from earlier experimental procedures carried out by him and involving feeding cats in the presence of anxiety evoking stimuli. Wolpe proposed physiological explanations of learning and unlearning and adopted the term reciprocal inhibition introduced by the physiologist Sherrington (1947) for 'all situations in which the elicitation of one response appears to bring about a decrement in the strength of evocation of a simultaneous response' (Wolpe 1958, *Psychotherapy by Reciprocal Inhibition*, Stanford University Press: 29). The procedure devised for the treatment of human anxiety consisted of the following steps: (1) clients are asked to make up a list of situations which are capable of frightening, disturbing, distressing or embarrassing them. These stimuli are then ordered on a hierarchy with the most disturbing items placed at the top and the least disturbing at the bottom of the list; (2) the second step involves the pairing of relaxation with each scene from the hierarchy starting with the least arousing items first. The therapist does not proceed up the hierarchy until the client ceases to report anxiety for the item presented. The assumption made to justify using imaginational rather than real life (*in vivo*) exposure was that imagined situations are capable of producing equivalent anxiety responses. It is therefore predicted that, if the client learns to experience relaxation rather than anxiety while imagining each scene from the hierarchy, the benefit would transfer to real life situations. There is ample evidence to support the efficacy of systematic desensitization but the processes contributing to change are unlikely to be those postulated by Wolpe (Kazdin & Wilson 1978; Rachman & Wilson 1980). When the effects of the various processes making up systematic desensitization were partialled out, it was found that relaxation was not necessary to its efficacy, neither was it necessary to keep anxiety at low levels, leaving exposure the only identified efficacious ingredient in the treatment package. In addition, flooding, another form of exposure based treatment, violated one of the basic assumptions of systematic desensitization by submitting clients to prolonged exposure to high intensity anxiety eliciting stimuli to good effect (Leitenberg 1976; Mathews 1978).

Exposure therapy. This form of therapeutic manipulation is now carried out routinely in imagination as well as *in vivo* for anxiety based disorders. The way in which frightening events are presented varies from choosing items ranked highest on a hierarchy to those placed lowest, with all points in between considered acceptable. Longer exposures have been found experimentally to be more effective than shorter ones and the close spacing of sessions (massed practice) has also been found to be an important determinant of good outcome (Emmelkamp 1982).

Relaxation therapy. While behaviour therapists originally used relaxation training as part and parcel of systematic desensitization, it has been accepted gradually as a form of treatment on its own. In a review of controlled studies investigating the efficacy of relaxation training, Glaister (1982) concluded that it was an effective method of fear reduction in its own right. Unfortunately, the studies reviewed were not easy to assess because some reports omitted procedural details while others reported on markedly different methods of training relaxation. Some tentative comparisons between different procedural variables relating to relaxation training have been initiated, but more are needed before one is in a strong position to recommend one type of relaxation training over another (Borkovec & Sides 1979; Lehrer & Woolfolk 1984).

Changing operants

The principles of operant conditioning are those which describe the relationship between behaviour and environmental events, that is, the antecedents and consequences which influence an individual's responses. Environmental events or stimuli known to influence behaviour can include physical features of the environment, an individual's own behaviour or the behaviour of others. Such stimuli can precede or follow operants. When the presentation of a stimulus increases a response the stimulus is called a positive reinforcer. On the other hand, stimuli which decrease behaviour are known as negative reinforcers. Behaviour is also decreased by the withholding of positive reinforcers. In practice, procedures based on operant conditioning are primarily procedures involving the contingent administration of positive reinforcing consequences.

Positive reinforcers. A classic example of the use of positive reinforcers to encourage non-pathological behaviour and eliminate pathological behaviour is the study carried out by Ayllon and Azrin (1968), who set aside an entire chronic ward of a mental hospital for a series of experiments in which rewards were given for desirable behaviour, such as those relating to self-care, but denied for symptomatic behaviour such as social withdrawal or engaging in bizarre, aimless activities. The rewards were plastic tokens which could be exchanged for special privileges such as listening to records or going to see a film. Operant conditioning behaviour therapy has been carried out widely with children, probably because much of the behaviour of children is subjected to the control of others, at home and at school. The range of children's problems tackled by operant procedures is very broad indeed, including such conditions as enuresis, thumb-sucking, aggression, tantrums, hyperactivity, disruptive classroom behaviour, poor school performance, asthmatic attacks and convulsive disorders (Doleys & Bruno 1982; Ruggles & LeBlanc 1982; Sulzer-Azaroff & Pollack 1982).

Negative reinforcers. The imposition of aversive consequences as a therapeutic tool has created an ethical dilemma for health professionals, whose commitment is to the general welfare of their client. Society also frowns upon the intentional infliction of pain or other unpleasant consequences unless it is done under certain well specified conditions and at the hands of responsible agents. Rimm and Masters (1979) cautioned that aversive techniques have the inherent power to cause physical or psychological harm, if used incorrectly. Their admonition extended to other techniques which may stress clients unduly, such as the flooding procedure mentioned earlier. In 1977, *Behaviour Therapy*, the journal of the Association for Advancement of Behavior Therapy, published *Ethical Issues for Human Services* to provide safeguards regarding the safety and rights of clients. In accordance with these, it is considered important for therapists who contemplate aversive techniques to obtain the client's informed consent, making sure that he/she knows that such consent may be withdrawn even after treatment has begun. When clients are unable to give informed consent because they are, for instance, mentally or physically handicapped, psychotic or too young, legal representation should be arranged for them before a decision to use aversion therapy is arrived at. Reflecting the reservations expressed by both professional and lay public, the *Journal of Behavior Therapy and Experimental Psychiatry* (Pergamon) warns its contributors that, 'manuscripts reporting the use of aversive or punishment procedures will generally not be accepted if non-aversive procedures have previously been shown to be effective for the target behavior and/or clinical populations concerned. Such manuscripts will be considered only if the aversive procedure has overwhelming advantages and is free of undesirable side-effects.'

By way of summary, a number of behaviour therapy procedures derive from two types of learning, namely respondent (or classical) conditioning and operant conditioning. These theoretical systems for the interpretation of learning have evolved from experimental studies carried out by psychologists. The major differences between respondent and operant conditioning are seen in that the primary result of respondent conditioning is a change in the power of a stimulus to elicit a reflexive response, while operant conditioning produces a change in the frequency of the response emitted or a change in some aspect of the response such as its intensity, speed or magnitude.

Social learning. Classical and operant conditioning theories have been criticized widely for their inability to explain adequately the acquisition of novel responses and complex skills such as language and other aspects of social development. They also fail to account for the role of language and thinking in behaviour control and evidence which shows that individuals learn by simply observing others. Modelling, imitation and observational learning are terms often used interchangeably for learning or behaviour change dependent on the observation of others. Modelling methods in behaviour therapy are recent in origin and attributed to the influence of Bandura (1969, 1971). The models used in these procedures include therapists or others who can demonstrate the target behaviour appropriately. Modelling techniques have proved to be effective with a variety of populations presenting with different problems. For instance, Matson (1981) found participant modelling effective with mentally retarded adults who were excessively fearful of participating in community based activities. Participant modelling includes demonstration plus participation by the client. In the Matson study, shopping for groceries was the target behaviour and therapists went over each step of the grocery shopping task before asking their subjects to perform it. Others helped by modelling techniques include persons of normal intelligence suffering from phobias, compulsions or lacking in social skills (Rachman & Hodgson 1980; Rimm & Masters 1979; Rosenthal & Bandura 1978).

Choosing a behaviour therapy programme

Criteria for selecting the programme

Cormier and Cormier (1985) proposed some criteria to be considered in selecting therapeutic strategies. These included:
1 Therapist characteristics and preferences.
2 Documentation for strategies.
3 Environmental factors.
4 Nature of client's problem.
5 Client's characteristics and preferences.

Therapist characteristics and preferences. The trained behaviour therapist has learned a wide range of behavioural procedures and is able to offer clients a number of alternative treatment plans. If the therapist prefers one method over another, the reasons for such a preference should be shared with the client concerned.

Documentation. Since there is an emphasis among practitioners of behaviour therapy on evaluating the efficacy of therapy, the available literature relating to the effectiveness of various procedures is well developed and its assimilation is an essential part of their training and constant up-dating. However, it will sometimes be unavoidable that experimental findings are not available to support a particular procedure. In this case the therapist is expected to assume responsibility for judging on the basis of experience. The therapist's experience is in turn invaluable in developing hypotheses to be scientifically tested.

Nature of client's problem. The behaviour therapist is expected to assume responsibility for suggesting strategies that are based upon the previous analysis of the client's problem. The first section of this chapter gave an overview of tried and tested methods used to affect overt behaviour and the next two chapters aim to provide further insights into the behaviour therapist's therapeutic repertoire.

Client characteristics and preferences. In the previous chapter, it was stressed that client and therapist need to develop a common language to communicate effectively with each other. This type of open communication should also influence decisions regarding the choice of intervention. In this way, the therapist can provide reasoned and reasonable alternatives which can be considered by the client before starting on a treatment programme. A comprehensive evaluation of the client as was suggested earlier ensures that the client's total context is understood before any action is taken. Client preferences, value systems, strength and weakness need to be realistically considered before a commitment is made to any course of action.

Environmental factors Both clients and therapists may be restricted by constraints placed on their respective environment. For instance, time constraints may be placed on both of them necessitating a brief and simple intervention. On the other hand, a client may need additional time and support from a therapist, if she/he is known to be of limited intelligence and/or placed in a particularly unrewarding environment.

The above criteria are consistent with the code of ethics embodied in *Ethical Issues for Human Services* (Association for Advancement of Behaviour Therapy 1977) mentioned earlier. They ensure that the client is able to give informed consent to work towards goals which she/he has had a hand in choosing by using sound methods which were also explained and decided on after discussion.

Choosing a programme for Mrs A

Therapist's formulation of Mrs A's problem

The client presented with a clinical picture consistent with a diagnosis of agoraphobia (Mathews, Gelder & Johnston 1981; Thorpe & Burns 1983) in that she avoided a number of specific situations away from home such as going into crowded shops, church, the bank, as well as visiting friends. Increasing distance and time away from home contributed to her distress. A trusted companion (one or the other of her daughters) helped her venture into the feared situations. She appeared to have learned to expect negative consequences during an unhappy and bewildering childhood and an early tumultuous marriage. A number of physical illnesses exacerbated hypochondriacal preoccupations. The marked avoidance of many everyday situations was considered to be the most problematical area of Mrs A's life as it decreased its quality considerably. Mrs A's reasons for seeking help at that time appeared to be the departures of her older daughters and her wish to make a new life for herself since her other children needed her less.

Programme. The teaching clinic to which the client was referred is conducting research into agoraphobics' responses to behavioural group programmes. Therefore, she was offered the opportunity to join a new group which was scheduled to start within a short period of time. The programme which was described to Mrs A during the interview reported in the previous chapter was originally piloted with agoraphobic clients on an individual basis and subsequently with a small group of clients. Details of the development of the programme are reported elsewhere (Liddell, Hughes & Plotz 1983). Briefly, the programme was conceptualized as an educational package whereby emphasis is placed on the understanding of anxiety as comprising a loose coupling of three systems (Lang 1969; Rachman 1978) and the relationship between the model and the coping strategies taught – relaxation, thought/stopping restructuring and the selection of realistic and practical goals to overcome avoidance. The aim and structure of the programme were presented simply to the client by the therapist at the end of the interview.

A number of practical and scientific considerations influenced the design of the programme. The efficacy of exposure procedures has already been discussed in relation to anxiety based disorders. The treatment of choice for agoraphobics is widely recognized to be exposure *in vivo* (Chambless & Goldstein 1982; Emmelkamp 1982; Mathews, Gelder & Johnston 1981; Thorpe & Burns 1982). Emmelkamp (1982) described two major variants of exposure *in vivo* successfully conducted with agoraphobic clients; self-controlled exposure which maximizes control and efficacy and prolonged exposure with therapist present, at least, during the early stages of treatment. It was decided to adopt the first option, on the grounds that it would answer the needs of busy clinicians concerned with cost/benefit issues,

issues regarding generalization of treatment sessions into the client's own environment and the development of self-efficacy in those clients. The decision to make the programme intensive and short was influenced by the fact that few clients remain in therapy more than a few sessions. In a comprehensive review of studies pertaining to premature termination of psychotherapy, Garfield (1978) found that the majority of the clients surveyed were in therapy for less than ten sessions. There is no reason to believe that the drop-out rate is less for behaviour therapy, since Barlow and Wolfe (1981) estimated a drop-out rate of approximately a third. Two separate evaluations of the programme demonstrated its efficacy (Liddell, Mackay, Dawe, Galitura, Hearn & Walsh-Doran 1986; Mackay & Liddell 1986).

Targets for self-exposure. Before leaving the clinic, Mrs A was asked to make up a hierarchy of her particular phobic situations and to rank them from very easy to very difficult. She was instructed to follow a method similar to that devised by Mathews *et al.* (1981) and describe two situations, one of which produced little or no anxiety while the other was to be the most difficult situation imaginable. She was then asked to bisect the interval between these situations and find a situation which was half-way between the two extremes and so on and so forth until she had a list of fifteen situations for planning a programme of self-exposure.

Group session 1. Sessions lasted approximately two hours each. A group leader steered the sessions but the clients were also subdivided into smaller groups of three to a therapist for task-oriented work. During small group work the hierarchy was reviewed by the therapist concerned, to see that it included items that clients could target for exposure more than once a week as well as situations which could be realistically initiated by them. From the resultant hierarchy, clients were instructed to choose one or two goals for exposure during the following week under the understanding that it was more important to be able to do less items more often than more items fewer times; three times a week for each goal was suggested as a minimum frequency for exposure. It was stressed that repeated exposure would enable them to cope with and tolerate their anxiety feelings, which would diminish eventually. The goals chosen for the following week were abstracted on to a sheet and clients were asked to record the frequency of having attempted their goal(s) and the length of time stayed in the situation (see p. 132). Goals were chosen from the lower levels of the hierarchy but clients were asked to choose goals which generated, at least, a little anxiety. A fear thermometer of 0 to 10 was used as a way of communicating anxiety feeling regarding each item and subjective ratings of two to four were generally accepted for initial exposure.

Relaxation training was conducted in the manner advocated by Bernstein and Borkovec (1973) and clients were asked to practise daily for, at least, twenty minutes. They were told that relaxation training had helped a number of people to decrease the physical signs of anxiety but that not everyone benefited from learning to relax physically. They were informed that they would also be given other strategies to help them cope with anxiety so that they could eventually find the best one for themselves or alternatively use different strategies according to the situation or according to how they showed anxiety was prominent at that particular time. These strategies, as well as the way in which client progress was evaluated, will be discussed in the following chapters.

Changing covert responses

This chapter addresses the legitimacy of methods which are aimed at problems caused by certain types of covert behaviour. It is agreed that a thorough assessment of any behaviour to be changed involves an understanding of its manifestation in three response systems, namely – somatic, cognitive and motoric. Avoidance behaviour reflects the overt aspect of anxiety alone. It is evident that phenomena other than avoidance take place when a person avoids a situation which is reacted to positively by most people. It follows that, in principle at least, anxiety can also be treated cognitively or physiologically and that there is not only one treatment possibility for any one problem. Treatments addressed to faulty cognition did not appear as serious contenders to the more orthodox conditioning therapies until the 1970s. Therefore, cognitive techniques have had less time to demonstrate their efficacy than the others.

Early behaviourists had hoped to be able to advance psychology as a science by attempting to predict responses as a function of stimuli, hence S-R psychology. Unfortunately this strict functionalist approach proved of limited value in predicting behaviour, although it is still accepted unchanged by groups of radical behaviour analysts whose conceptual approach to the understanding of behaviour and its subsequent modification goes under the name of *applied behaviour analysis* (Ch. 1). The neobehaviourism of Eysenck

(1982) offered behaviour therapists an alternative solution, one which had permeated general psychology as *conceptual behaviourism* (Valentine 1982). It became necessary to postulate some types of processes intervening between stimulus and response if psychologists were to increase their understanding of human behaviour. These processes, although conceptually necessary, cause problems to the scientist because they are not directly observable. This state of affairs is not unknown in other sciences, for instance physics. Valentine contrasted two views of conceptual behaviourism, one in which the constructs postulated must be tied to direct observations, with a more accommodating one in which the constructs need to be related to some observations but not exclusively.

Eysenck (1982) proposed organismic variables to modulate the effects of stimulus and response. These variables fitted into a well-defined dimensional model of personality in which the dimensions of extraversion and neuroticism were first identified, followed later by a third dimension of psychoticism (Eysenck & Eysenck 1976). It was suggested by Eysenck and Rachman (1965) that extraversion would be implied in individuals' responses to a conditioning treatment. However, Beech (1969), reviewing the evidence to support this claim, was forced to conclude: 'The case for the relationship between the results of behaviour therapy and this aspect of the personality of the patient is rather weak' (Beech 1969 *Changing Man's Behavior*, Penguin: 243). This lack of support, no doubt, had some bearing on the observations of Kendall *et al.* (1981) that the neobehaviouristic (S-R) model had little influence on the behaviour therapy research published in the 1970s. At the same time few clinicians would deny the importance that individual client characteristics have on the development and maintenance of any behaviour, be it problematic or not.

Norton, Dinardo and Barlow (1983) advocated a similar approach to that of Eysenck, in suggesting that one should consider individual fear response patterns within the three-systems model of anxiety (cognitive/subjective, physiological and behavioural) to match individuals with treatment to increase efficacy. There is encouraging support in the literature that matching a client's fear response pattern to its logically prescribed method has enhanced therapeutic efficacy (Mackay & Liddell 1986; Öst, Johansson & Jerremalm 1982). However, in view of the complexity of human behaviour, it is likely that the search for relevant client variables will continue for some time to come.

Covert responses

It is universally accepted that human beings have great potential for cognitive activities. This is reflected in various ways such as their ability to solve complex problems, learn languages and create imaginary worlds. Human beings' potential for thinking and imagining can, under certain circumstances, be to their detriment.

The search for predictable and predicting intervening variables

Wolpe (1958), who relied heavily on unobservable imagery for his therapeutic approach, conceptualized imagery as specific neural events which have equivalence with objects of the real world. In other words, a response to an imagined fearful stimulus has the same physiological qualities as if the stimulus was perceived *in vivo*. Lang (1977), influenced by the psychology of information processing, reassessed and expanded this view by conceptualizing imagery thus: 'We have suggested that the narrow definition of the image, as an internal stimulus, is theoretically inadequate and of limited practical utility. We proposed alternatively that the emotional image in the brain is a propositional construct, a finite structure made up of a stimulus and response elements which are under limited instructional control' (Lang 1977, Imagery in therapy, *Behavior Therapy*: 882). Lang and his collaborators have shown repeatedly that it is possible to measure components of imagining through concurrent physiological monitoring – for instance, heart rate –

enabling reliable observations of private events. In this way, an inferred concept is tied intimately to direct observations making orthodox scientific studies possible.

A recent study, directed at another different intervening variable, is given to illustrate the problems encountered by psychologists who wish to remain scientific while investigating covert events. The investigation aimed to throw light on *worry* – a well-known human experience. Borkovec and his collaborators developed an interest in this phenomenon as a result of their studies with insomniacs who were invariably found to be worrying their nights away (Borkovec, Robinson, Pruzinsky & De Pree 1983). This group of researchers spent a year in weekly exploratory meetings set aside to conceptualize the nature of worrying. To this effect, they drew from personal experience, the available relevant literature and clinical interviews with known chronic worriers. As a result of their discussions, it became clear to them that the task of defining worry was not an easy one and would take them considerable time and effort. It also became obvious that the nature and process of worry needed to be distinguished from other emotionally-related concepts such as fear/anxiety, and from other cognitive activities such as mental problem-solving. After careful consideration, they proposed the following definition: 'Worry is a chain of thoughts and images, negatively affect-laden and relatively uncontrollable. The worry process represents an attempt to engage in mental problem-solving on an issue whose outcome is uncertain but contains the possibility of one or more negative outcomes. Consequently, worry relates closely to fear processes' (Borkovec *et al.* 1983 Preliminary exploration of worry: some characteristics and processes, *Behaviour Research and Therapy*: 10).

An initial test of the concept was carried out by asking a group of students of both sexes to complete a number of self-report inventories including measures of anxiety and fears, depression and latency to sleep-onset. As a measure of worry, subjects were asked to estimate what percentage of a typical day they experienced worry and general tension on a

100-point scale. The results showed no sex difference in worry or general tension. Therefore, correlations with the other measures were computed for the total sample to reveal that magnitude of reported worrying related to numerous fears and anxiety, depressions and delayed sleep-onset. A second study was designed to obtain more information about the worrying process by means of a questionnaire. The questionnaire was made up of items which assessed mood, content of worries, autonomic perception while worrying, temporal aspects of content of worry and controllability of worries. The results showed that worriers feel anxious when worrying, academic issues were most often worried about (not too unexpected in a student population), some awareness of muscle tension was experienced during worrying, worry content was primarily located in the future and, finally, worriers had less control over their worries than non-worriers. The first two surveys were followed by a study conducted in a laboratory and designed to compare worriers and non-worriers on affect and physiological activity under a number of specified conditions. Many useful findings emerged from the laboratory study, one of which indicated that worriers and non-worriers differed in their ability to focus on attention tasks – worriers reporting a higher frequency of negative intrusive thoughts in the laboratory than non-worriers. However, autonomic activity as measured by heart-rate did not differentiate between the two groups. The authors qualified this finding by suggesting that physiological measures other than heart-rate may have been more appropriate and should be used in future studies as markers of worry. The study exemplified a scientific approach to covert events by showing how a group of research psychologists defined and manipulated private events inside and outside the laboratory and their attempts to relate covert responding to observable dimensions.

Pathological covert responses

Initially, most psychiatric syndromes treated by behaviour therapists were viewed primarily in their overt behavioural manifestations. But it did not take too long for behaviourists to attempt to relate motoric behaviour to cognitive or physiological components of these syndromes. Two characteristic psychiatric syndromes will be discussed. The first – *obsessive-compulsive neurosis* – has been known for many generations of psychiatrists, although accounting for a small proportion of the total treated population. The other condition is *depression*, a common and pervasive symptom which can be seen as a problem on its own or as part of other syndromes.

Obsessive-compulsive responses. It is commonly accepted that the term obsession refers to the thought or cognitive component of the disorder while compulsion is used for the overt behaviour, for instance, the excessive washing and checking engaged in by some of those who present with the disorder. Behaviour therapists have improved prognosis for obsessive-compulsives dramatically by treating them with a form of response prevention, that is, by preventing clients directly or indirectly from engaging in their compelling ritualistic behaviour (Beech & Vaughn 1978; Meyer, Levy & Schnurer 1974; Rachman & Hodgson 1980; Sturgis & Meyer 1980). A number of research studies offered support for the often made clinical observation that compulsions were instrumental in reducing anxiety although this was not evident in every case of compulsive behaviour (Beech & Liddell 1974; Rachman & Hodgson 1980). Initially, as would be expected, obsessions received less attention than compulsions from behaviour therapists. Some hoped that changes in the frequency of overt compulsive behaviour would result in decreased obsessional thinking. Unfortunately, the relationship between obsessions and compulsions proved more elusive than had been envisaged by some.

Akhtar, Wig, Varma, Pershad and Verma (1975) carried out a phenomenological study of the symptoms of a large number of obsessional-compulsive patients by collecting information from semi-structured psychiatric interviews. They defined obsession in the following way: 'an anxiety-provoking psychic phenomenon that recurs in spite of the patient's resisting it and regarding it as alien to himself and, at times, clearly absurd' (Akhtar *et al.* 1975, A phenomenological analysis of symptoms in obsessive-compulsive neurosis, *British Journal of Psychiatry*: 343). The results showed that approximately one quarter of the sample of obsessive-compulsive patients interviewed presented with obsessive thinking without any form of compulsions. They found five forms of obsessions sufficient to categorize most of the obsessions described by their subjects. These were classified and defined in the following way: (1) obsessive doubt by 'an inclination not to believe that a completed task has been accomplished satisfactorily'; (2) obsessive thinking by 'a seemingly endless thought chain, usually one pertaining to future events'; (3) obsessive impulse by 'a powerful urge to carry out actions which may be trivial or socially disruptive or even assaultive'; (4) obsessive fear by 'a fear of losing self-control and thus inadvertently committing a socially embarrassing act'; (5) obsessive image by 'the persistence before the mind's eye of something seen, usually recently' (Akhtar *et al.* 1975: 343–4). It follows that obsessions can present themselves as the main problem and that they can be identified and classified with some degree of confidence. Rachman (1971a) proposed a model for obsessional ruminations in which they were represented as noxious stimuli to which clients fail to habituate. This model helped greatly in developing some of the specific treatment for obsessions which will be discussed later.

Depression. The recognition of depression as a human problem is as old as the world itself. This is evident from the writings of all literate civilizations from the ancient Greeks to the present. Several views have been advanced to enable a classification. These views can usefully be examined under three headings: a unitary view, a dualistic view and a pluralistic view. Those who hold the unitary view assume that depression has an underlying unity which ranges from grief to severe clinical depression. The dualistic view presents depression as dichotomous with one depression labelled psychotic, endogenous or somatic, while the other is viewed as a neurotic reaction, exogenous or precipitated by a significant loss. An example of a pluralist view is seen when psychotic and neurotic depressions are respectively sub-divided according to known aetiological and/or prognostic factors. Another pluralist approach is to label depression according to certain developmental milestones or character-istics of the depressed themselves, i.e., childhood or adolescent depression, menopausal depression or masked depression. Clinicians usually have some rule of thumb for differentiating between clinical and non-clinical depression. The author of this book would look for a mood change indicating depressed feeling, sadness, feeling blue, low or gloomy and low self-esteem. In addition, at least six of the following ten complaints would confirm the diagnosis: complaint of thinking slowly, anorexia, insomnia, constipa-tion, feeling tired, decreased ability to concentrate, suicidal ideas, weight loss, decreased sexual interest/activity, wringing of hands and pacing. As would be expected in such a clinical picture, the list includes a mixture of cognitive, physiological and motoric symptoms. These three aspects are also repre-sented in standardized and widely used scales to assess degrees of experienced depression such as the Beck Depression Inven-tory (BDI) (Beck, Ward, Mendelsohn, Mock and Erbaugh, 1961) and the Hamilton Rating Scale (Hamilton 1967).

In view of the divergences of opinion as to the number and types of depressions, it is not surprising to find many competing explanations in the vast literature pertaining to this subject. Psychological explanations are of recent origins and tentative. Williams (1984) gave a good history of the development of psychological thinking on the subject. He reviewed orthodox behavioural models based on low rates of response-contingent reinforcement as well as more recent and complex models which favour a more cognitive approach to depression. Some aspects of these models will be taken up again later with a discussion of cognitive treatment for depression; suffice to say that the essence of these models is to suggest various forms of cognitive loss of control and distortions reflected in such concepts as negative attributions and expectations, negative automatic thoughts, systematic logical errors and depressogenic schemata.

Methods of changing covert responses

Overt behaviour was the first target for change in the development of behavioural techniques but the first category of covert event to be recognised as useful in engineering change was imagery. An individual's capacity for producing imagery is manipulated in a number of ways. In systematic desensitization, it is used as the equivalent of objects or situations feared in the real world. The therapist systematically teaches the client muscular relaxation, then asks him/her to imagine an anxiety producing scene under the assumption that the relaxation response will replace anxiety and that this transfers to real-life situations. Prior to beginning exposure in imagination, clients are usually asked to recall scenes which elicit pleasant and relaxing feelings. Suitable scenes are often those of remembered holidays, set in quiet and peaceful environments such as the seaside on a warm and sunny day, in which clients were calm and contented. Clients are instructed to keep one or two such scenes in mind to be brought up as alternatives to the anxiety producing scenes and/or to facilitate physical relaxation.

Gurman (1973) described the successful treatment of a young man who sought help for anxiety which prevented him from presenting required research reports at graduate school seminars, by an ingenious use of imagery. The method was named *cue-controlled relaxation*. The subject was asked to imagine a personally pleasant and relaxing scene aloud. He was further requested to choose a catch-word for the scene and practise twice a day, for a period of ten minutes each practice, associating (conditioning) the catch-word with the feeling of calmness and relaxation brought on by the favoured scene. Once the connection was made, the client was instructed to use the catch-word whenever he felt anxious during *in vivo* exposure sessions. Gurman explained the positive therapeutic outcome obtained in the following way:

> The patient's subjective reports of his feelings and behavior in the present case suggested that while the graded *in vivo* exposures and the use of cue-controlled relaxation were both effective agents in reducing his anxiety, he experienced the latter as the more potent therapeutic ingredient. The patient's ability to effectively self-administer the cue (his catch-word) for anxiety-relief whenever he found it necessary in public-speaking situations fostered, according to the patient, a sense of self-control of his anxiety (Gurman 1973, Treatment of a case of public-speaking anxiety by *in vivo* desensitization and cue-controlled relaxation, *Journal of Behavior Therapy and Experimental Psychiatry*: 53).

In the middle 1960s Cautela developed a number of cognitive intervention procedures drawing primarily from operant conditioning principles. He worked under the assumption that covert events obey the same laws as overt events and that covert and overt events interact to influence each other. He shared the second assumption (interaction) with the majority of cognitive behaviour modifiers but the first assumption (homogeneity) set him apart from many other behaviour therapists. A typical way of explaining the approach to a new client is presented in Cautela's own words:

> Your undesired behaviors occur primarily because they are being maintained by the environment. The environment has many ways of influencing you. People in the environment may be rewarding, punishing, or ignoring you, and thereby maintaining a particular behavior. Your observation of what other people do and what happens to them also affects your behavior. These are just a few examples. By changing how the environment influences you, we can change your behavior. If you are rewarded for a desirable behavior, the desired behavior will increase. If you are punished for an undesired behavior, it will decrease. I shall teach you techniques in which you imagine

yourself or another person performing a particular behavior, and then you imagine the appropriate consequence. When you imagine your scene, it is important that you involve all your senses. If you are walking through the woods, imagine that you can feel the wind on your face, hear branches rubbing against one another, see the rays of sun filtering through the leaves, and smell the earth. Experience the movements in your body. The most critical part of your imagining is that you feel that you are actually experiencing the event rather than just seeing yourself (Cautela 1979, *Covert Conditioning*, Pergamon: 4).

Cautela listed six covert conditioning procedures which are consistent with known principles of learning – covert positive reinforcement, covert negative reinforcement, covert sensitization, covert extinction, covert modelling and covert response cost. Covert conditioning methods were found effective in a variety of problems including anxiety disorders, addicted behaviour, obsessive-compulsive behaviour, pain behaviour and sexual problems (Upper & Cautela 1979).

An increasingly large and diverse group of behaviour therapists subscribe to a cognitive behaviour therapy approach with varying degrees of commitment to learning principles. The main assumption unifying them is their belief in the importance of covert events in understanding and changing behaviour. These new cognitive behaviour therapists have developed techniques which can be classified under two broad headings, according to their prime function; the first of these techniques aims to decrease, stop or minimize unwanted thoughts, and the other aims to modify or change certain types of thinking.

Procedures to control thinking

Thought stopping. Wolpe (1958) recognized that a great deal of anxiety is due to persistent negative thoughts which are clearly out of proportion to the realities involved. He credited a colleague of his (J. G. Taylor) at the University of Cape Town for a *simple method for freeing patients from useless thoughts*. Patients who report intrusive negative thoughts are asked to close their eyes while verbalizing a typical unadaptive thought sequence. As this is taking place, the therapist shouts *STOP*! The procedure is repeated several times, each time, the therapist pointing out to the patient the fact that intrusive thoughts are actually stopped by the procedure. The patient is then instructed to stop his own thoughts by saying to himself *STOP*! subvocally. Wolpe altered the method for patients who did not respond readily to this procedure. Those patients were asked to try to keep their minds on pleasant thoughts and to press a buzzer, which was placed within their reach, every time they failed by letting through unpleasant thoughts. On hearing the buzzer, Wolpe would shout *STOP*! He evaluated the efficacy of the procedure by counting the frequency of buzzer presses over a period of fifteen minutes and noted a substantial decline after the first two or three minutes. As a result of clinical experience, he deemed thought stopping to be highly successful except in cases of 'chronic, well-defined obsessional ideas, and even with these, worth while amelioration is sometimes obtained' (Wolpe 1958, *Psychotherapy by Reciprocal Inhibition*, Stanford University Press: 201).

Some twenty years later, Tryon (1979) wrote a critical review of the research into the efficacy of thought stopping. She described other variations of the original technique implemented by clinicians over the years. These included the use of electric shock in place of a buzzer, clients snapping themselves with a thick rubber band on their wrist and clients counting backwards from ten to zero instead of saying *STOP*! She found the case for thought stopping techniques difficult to prove because of variations in the procedures investigated and because thought stopping has often been used in combination with other procedures, making it impossible to assess its unique contribution to positive outcome. In one of the few studies to include a control group, Stern, Lipsedge and Marks (1973) compared the effectiveness of a tape-recorded thought stopping session with another type of tape-recorded session in which the clients were to imagine a neutral scene rather than the unwanted thought before *STOP*! was vocalized. Results indicated that only four of the eleven clients treated by the traditional thought stopping technique improved significantly; clients were split as to their preference for the experimental or control treatments.

Habituation procedures. Rachman and Hodgson (1980) viewed thought stopping as a type of dismissal-training method of uncertain practical utility, with regard to obsessions. As an alternative, they proposed an habituation procedure based on Rachman's earlier definition of obsession as noxious stimulus to which clients fail to habituate (Rachman 1971a). The technique involves asking clients to deliberately form the unwanted thoughts and to retain them for prolonged periods of time, without carrying out any form of neutralizing activities. Emphasis is placed on self-management and clients are urged to practise the newly acquired skills outside the clinic. Milby, Meredith and Rice (1981) adapted the method with one obsessive-compulsive patient who presented with checking behaviour as well as obsessions. They made videotapes of the patient being questioned closely on her obsessive thoughts, as to their content, variations of obsessive theme along with feared consequences. The tapes were edited to make separate tapes of each of the individual obsessional themes reported by the patient. Discussions lasted approximately two minutes and were repeated approximately thirty times during a one-hour training session. After six weekly sessions of exposure to the tapes, the patient's obsessions had decreased substantially and her improvement was maintained after seventeen months.

Gurnani and Vaughn (1981) treated five obsessive-compulsive patients, whose prominent symptoms were intrusive unacceptable thoughts, with another variation of an habituation procedure. These subjects were also treated on a weekly exposure schedule but received three sessions only. During the first interview, the troublesome thoughts were associated to a key phrase agreed on by patient and therapist. The key phrase included the essentials of the thought and was capable of evoking the feelings and images associated with it. During each session, the patient was asked to repeat the key phrase without pausing for a period of one hour. Distress ratings and frequency counts of the obsessions were used to evaluate outcome. Frequency of obsessions went down significantly, with the reduction being most marked in the first session, but the level of distress stayed the same or increased over sessions, lending only partial support for the model on which the treatment was based.

Restructuring thinking. Meichenbaum and his colleagues demonstrated that what people say to themselves, while performing certain tasks, can affect their performance. For instance, after giving a reaction time task to normal subjects, they discovered that these subjects enhanced their task performance by inventing cognitive games. On the other hand, adult schizophrenic and impulsive children, who were exhibiting attentional deficits, appeared unable to do likewise. Following from these observations, the researchers developed self-instructional training procedures which improved the performance of schizophrenic and impulsive children (Meichenbaum & Cameron 1973; Meichenbaum & Goodman 1971). Meichenbaum (1975) described self-instructional training as having three stages. The first two stages – definition of problem behaviour and conceptualization of presenting problem(s) – are common to all behaviour therapy programmes, but the third, training in modification of self-statement to produce more adaptive cognition, is unique to the self-instructional training method. Rehearsal of coping skills can be said to be the essence of Meichenbaum's stress inoculation training. By this type of cognitive rehearsal, clients learn to function in spite of their anxiety rather than learn to loose the anxiety completely. Initially, client and therapist work at finding positive self-statements which will assist in dealing with anxiety. In Meichenbaum's own words, the functions of the self-statements should be to encourage them to: '(a) assess the reality of the situation; (b) control negative, self-defeating, anxiety-engendering ideation; (c) acknowledge, use, and possibly relabel the anxiety they were experiencing; (d) 'psych' themselves up to perform the task; (e) cope with the intense fear they might experience; and (f) reinforce themselves for having coped' (Meichenbaum 1975 Self-instructional methods, in Kanfer & Goldstein, *Helping People to Change*, Pergamon). The stress inoculation procedure is usually used in conjunction with relaxation training and exposure *in vivo*.

McMullin and Casey (1975) drew from the work of other behaviour therapists and, more specifically, from the *rational-emotive therapy* created by Ellis (1962) by emphasing cognition above all. They called their approach *cognitive restructuring therapy*. As part of this approach, they proposed a different type of ABC analysis than that carried out by other behaviour therapists (see Ch. 2). In this model, A stands for the situation, B for the thought and C for the reaction. Unlike the S-R model, A (the situation/stimulus) does not cause C (the emotion/response) but B (attitude about A) does. It was assumed that, when attitudes regarding certain situations are unrealistic and irrational, a change in the attitudes causing the negative emotion would result in the gradual disappearance of the unwanted emotion. Forty-five examples of thoughts that cause problems were given by the authors and include such irrational beliefs as:

1. People must love me or I will be miserable. 5. My emotions can't be controlled. 10. I can't stand the way others act. 15. I should help everyone who needs it. 20. There is a magic cure for my problems. 25. I am inferior. 30. One must always be sure to decide. 35. There is a secret, terrible part of me that controls me. 40. I have no problems. 45. Will power alone can solve all my problems (McMullin & Casey 1975, *Talk Sense to Yourself*! Counselling Research Institute, CO.: 52–3).

A *cognitive restructuring therapy* programme consists of, first, identifying problem thoughts to determine whether they are or are not irrational and untrue. When a cognition is found to be irrational and untrue, clients are encouraged to gradually substitute them by practising with alternative rational modes of thinking, *until they have learned to talk sense to themselves.*

Changing irrational thoughts is also emphasized by Beck in his *cognitive therapy* for depression. From Williams' (1984) review of psychological treatments for depressions, we find examples of habitual errors identified as depressive and targeted for change by Beck and others like him. These include:

> dichotomous thinking (black/white, all or nothing thinking), where there is no perceived middle path – just the extremes; selective abstraction, the selecting out of small parts of a situation and ignoring others, e.g. a tutor's report on your essay gives much praise, but mentions at one point that the Introduction was too long. 'He doesn't like my essay' would be selective abstraction; arbitrary inference, where a conclusion is inferred from irrelevant evidence, e.g. you phone your boy/girl friend and no one answers '(S)he's probably out with another partner' would be arbitrary inference (if inferred on those grounds alone); overgeneralisation, to conclude from one specific negative event that another negative event is thereby more likely, e.g. failure at maths means failure at everything; catastrophising, to think the very worst of a situation. Each of the above examples would suffice (Williams 1984, *The Psychological Treatment of Depression,* Free Press: 111).

Beck uses many techniques, not all of which are cognitive in nature, to effect cognitive changes. Broadly speaking, his procedure involves eliciting the thoughts likely to maintain depression, discussing with the client evidence for or against the unwarranted interpretations and, finally, setting up experiments in the form of homework by which the patient tests the validity of his/her interpretation until the problem beliefs are dispelled. Beck's approach dates back to the early 1960s but his pioneering work was not taken up widely by other behaviour therapists until the 1970s (Whitehead 1979;

Williams 1984). Although it seems unlikely that all depressions will respond to a psychological approach, cognitive methods have already made a strong impact and their application is likely to increase even more in the foreseeable future.

In summary, this chapter has attempted to show the development and acceptance of the use of cognitive methods by behaviour therapists. Some of these so-called cognitive methods are used in conjunction with other non-cognitive behavioural methods, others as the prime therapy. As a group of techniques, they have not had as much time to demonstrate their utility as the methods discussed in the previous chapter. On the other hand, they have shown utility with a range of problems encountered in the clinic, including conditions which were not tackled initially by behaviour therapists, such as obsessions and depression.

Mrs A's cognitions

During the interview, Mrs A was questioned about her overt behaviour, that is, the types of situation she avoided due to anxiety and the degree of that avoidance, how she recognized her anxiety feelings physiologically and how she construed her own behaviour and that of other people. From this initial interview, many examples of her cognitions are found. For instance, when she recalled her thoughts during a panic attack which made her return home after having tried to go out on her own: 'I'd say – My God I'm going to die, I'm dying! I'm never going to make it, home seemed so far away' (p. 29). During her account of her childhood panic attacks at school and of physiological sensations, the therapist asked: 'Did you think then that you had a heart condition?' To which the client answered: 'Oh yes, I was sure of it and I probably still am. I would dwell on my heart and I'd be feeling my pulse. That was the one thing on my mind' (p. 34). Regarding her thoughts about living with a violent alcoholic husband, she said: 'It became so bad that I was living in fear for my life' (p. 37). Later she gave as the reason for staying with her husband twenty years: 'I was afraid he would take the children. You know he had me down to such a low level. I had no self-confidence. I never had much anyway but the bit I had, I had lost' (p. 43). Before she finally separated from her husband, she was able to say: 'He tried very hard, but I found I had no faith in him whatsoever' (p. 44). Her thoughts about the possibility of future involvements were summed up by: 'I did date a couple of men, like at house parties and things like that, but I find I'm really not that interested in anything serious. I don't know if I could handle it again' (p. 46). Her attitudes to her medical advisers were reflected by (first psychiatrist): 'he's not very good'; (second psychiatrist) 'he doesn't talk to me very much. I don't even believe he knows about this agoraphobia'; (GP who preceded the referring GP) 'I lost a bit of faith' (p. 48). Her current preoccupation about her health was voiced as: 'Well right now I'm worried about this pain and cancer and things like that' (p. 50). Later she brought up the same preoccupation in this way: 'I am worried because I don't feel well lately – I also have back pain. I worry about it then I say, what the heck if I have cancer, I go and I'm still here' (p. 51).

Mrs A voiced many negative thoughts about herself and other people along with recurrent hypochondriacal preoccupations. During the first group session of the agoraphobic treatment programme, clients were taught relaxation to help decrease the unpleasant bodily feelings of anxiety and more will be said about that aspect of the programme in the next chapter. During the second session, clients were asked to make a closer analysis of their negative and unadaptive thinking than had been possible during the initial interview. At the time of treatment, Mrs A found her hypochondriacal preoccupations most debilitating. She was asked to try to identify the types of situation in which they came. She thought that they occurred most often when she was alone, when she heard about someone else's illness or saw a television programme discussing health or illness. However, sometimes those thoughts seemed to come out of a clear blue sky and proved very difficult to get rid of, whatever she was doing at the time. As a consequence, she felt afraid, depressed and worried but also angry about the prospect of having to deal with doctors she had little confidence in. Very often, the hypochondriacal thoughts led to other negative thoughts about herself and her failure to lead a normal life.

It appeared that Mrs A had some recurrent thoughts about her health which had many obsessional characteristics while other thoughts were more in the nature of faulty beliefs needing restructuring. Sharing this understanding, she and her therapist explored ways to alter her negative cognition. She was taught a number of thought stopping strategies to help stop the hypochondriacal thoughts when they seemed compelling and out of control. She preferred the rubber band which she carried continually during the treatment programme and some weeks afterwards. Whenever she began to worry about her health, she snapped the elastic band and found the thought to decrease in its intensity. In addition, she set out a *worrying time*, a period of fifteen minutes in which she brought back into her consciousness her hypochondriacal or any other preoccupation without interruption. The method is similar to the habituation technique discussed earlier and was included in a self-help book for depression (Lewinsohn, Muñoz, Youngren & Zeiss 1978). She found that her thoughts were much less compelling after her worrying time and the negative feelings associated with them also decreased considerably after each session. The client also made an effort to be with company more often and not to look at television alone when a health/illness programme was shown.

The client's experiences had led her to expect the worst from herself and other people, doctors in particular. She was encouraged to think of the GP she had confidence in, as evidence that all medical practitioners were not bad and that she had probably been unlucky in the past. During her homework – self-paced exposure – she was given guidelines to change the thoughts which had discouraged her when she had panic attacks. She was asked to copy the shortened version of the rules given by Mathews, Gelder and Johnston (1981) to deal with panic, on both sides of a small card (5 × 3 in), learn them and take the card with her every time she left home. The rules are the following:

1 The feelings are normal bodily reactions.
2 They are not harmful.
3 Do not add frightening thoughts.
4 Describe what is happening.
5 Wait for fear to pass.
6 Notice when it fades.
7 It is an opportunity for progress.
8 Think of what you have done.
9 Plan what to do next.
10 Then start off slowly

(Mathews *et al.* 1981, *Agoraphobia: Nature and Treatment*, Guilford: 183).

Chapter 5

Changing physiological responses

The suggestion that it is advisable to consider information from three modes of responding is not really a revolutionary idea to psychologists. Valentine (1982) introduced the body-mind controversy, a perennial issue of academic psychology, by reminding the reader that the subject matter of psychology is widely thought to include conscious experience, behaviour and physiology. She goes on to say that psychologists – and many others before them – have puzzled over the particular relationship between physiology (more recently, neurophysiological processes) and consciousness. In other words, how can neurophysiological processes give rise to consciousness when each appears so different in kind? Are there two kinds of realities (body and mind) or just one? If one only, which one exists? If two, is one more important than the other? Which one? Valentine concluded her discussion of the mind-body issue in the following way:

> Epistemologically, there is an asymmetry between the subject's and the observer's perspective. Statements describing experiences are not identical in meaning to those describing physical phenomena, as can be seen from the example of a blind neurophysiologist who might have complete knowledge of the physiological basis of colour vision, and yet not know what it was like to see colour. Metaphysically, double aspect theory may be recommended. To the extent that descriptions

have an element of arbitrariness, pragmatism may be appropriate. Thus, psychologists may adopt different frameworks to suit different purposes, given that the demands of conceptual coherence and consistency with the empirical have been met (Valentine 1982, *Conceptual Issues in Psychology*, Allen and Unwin: 31).

Her conclusions vindicate the behaviour therapist who chooses to operate within a broad psychological spectrum rather than focus narrowly on one aspect of the client. On the other hand, a broad spectrum approach creates many kinds of intellectual problems, in particular, a need to define and understand the different aspects of human activities subsumed under conscious experience, behaviour and physiology as well as study their various interactions. It was pointed out earlier (Ch. 2) that behaviour therapists can gather their information by eliciting self-reports from clients, by directly observing them or by mechanically monitoring a relevant physiological function. This permits clients to be construed as tripartite organisms recognizable to all psychologists. A summary discussion concerning the three aspects making up what is supposed to be human nature follows, before approaching the problems caused by the particular make-up of human physiology.

Behaviour, consciousness and physiology

Behaviour as the subject of study of early behaviourists was limited to overt behaviour, that is, public events that could be reliably observed and measured. The focus on overt behaviour and the analysis of its relationship to stimulus made the evolution of a theory of behaviour possible. Resultant learning theories looked similar in quality to the theories of other sciences, fulfilling psychologists' aspirations of scientific respectability. The reluctance of radical behaviourists to give up this position is understandable in the light of the knowledge obtained by following a strictly behaviourist approach to the study of human behaviour.

The ideas of Popper and Kuhn, regarding the philosophy and history of science respectively, have greatly influenced psychologists of the post-war period (Churchland 1984; Valentine 1982). Popper concerned himself with differentiating scientific from non-scientific statements and, to achieve this, he made *falsifiability* the ultimate goal of all hypotheses testing. Kuhn, on the other hand, recognized the search for a paradigm as the impetus which moved every group of scientists, be they behavioural or physical scientists. Early stages in the development of a science are characterized by conflict between competing schools of thought while scientific maturity is recognized by paradigmatic agreement within which a true science is able to progress. Psychology has often been judged to be at the pre-paradigmatic stage when compared with the physical sciences. However, Valentine singled out behaviourism as coming,

> as close to the notion of paradigm as anything could. It seems particularly easy to specify its assumptions with respect to: (a) fundamentals – determinism, the analysis of behaviour in terms of stimuli and responses, behaviour as a function of conditioning history in terms of reinforcement contingencies, (b) subject matter – behaviour rather than experience, emphasis on learning rather than more cognitive (i.e. perception and thinking) or physiological components, (c) method – objective observation, introspection only as verbal report, progress from simple to complex forms of behaviour, (d) explanation – functional analysis with the emphasis on prediction and control, general laws, conditioning as a pre-theoretic model (Valentine 1982, *Conceptual Issues in Psychology*, Valentine: 87–8).

No wonder that it proved so difficult for behaviourists to abandon orthodox behaviourism and go back to the drawing board – this in spite of the fact that the limits of the approach were amply demonstrated in the clinic. Behavioural assessments were originally based on the overt-motoric aspect of behaviour but clinicians never stopped being confronted by clients' private experiences. They needed to choose between ignoring this aspect of behaviour or integrating it in the assessment and management problems presented to them. However, considering private experience cannot be done without making some assumptions regarding the nature of consciousness.

At the most basic level, consciousness can be viewed as experience or awareness. The *Oxford Concise Dictionary* defines it as 'totality of a person's thoughts and feelings'. It is usual to distinguish an aspect of consciousness which deals with sensory experiences from a higher order self-consciousness in which one is aware of one's awareness. In a contemporary introduction to the philosophy of the mind, Churchland (1984) explained the distinction in the following way:

> To be self-conscious is to have, at a minimum, knowledge of oneself. But this is not all. Self-consciousness involves knowledge not just of one's physical states, but knowledge of one's mental states specifically. Additionally, self-consciousness involves the same kind of continuously updated knowledge that one enjoys in one's continuous perception of the external world. Self-consciousness, it seems, is a kind of continuous apprehension of an inner reality, the reality of one's mental states and activities (Churchland 1984, *Matter and Consciousness*, The Massachusetts Institute of Technology Press: 73).

He goes on to say later, that self-consciousness 'has a very large *learned* component'. This assumption figured largely in the development of cognitive methods of behaviour change (Ch. 4). Introspection, which had been abandoned by earlier behaviourists, reappeared as a legitimate method of inquiry to obtain information relating to the verbal-cognitive mode of responding. Therefore, it is commonplace for behaviour therapists to ask their clients for ratings of anxiety or pain as well as descriptions of aversive thought contents and establish base lines of their frequency and intensity.

While a complete understanding of the relationship between consciousness and other aspects of the person remains problematic, the technology introduced by computers has provided researchers with means of simulating some of the features of conscious intelligence (artificial intelligence or AI for short) for scrutiny. The computer is sometimes used as a model to think of human beings as information processing systems. In the computer analogy, the physiological make-up is viewed as the hardware which is programmed to operate by a conscious software. At other times, computers are used to replicate and study certain specific types of cognitive activities.

While academic cognitive psychologists have, so far, made more progress in the understanding of cognitive (cold cognitions) as opposed to the affective (hot cognitions) aspect of consciousness, clinical psychologists deal more often with affects such as anxiety, depression, anger. An interesting debate relating to the relationship of cognition and affect is presently taking place in the scientific literature. The debate was stimulated by Zajonc (1980) in an article entitled 'Feeling and thinking: Preferences need no inference', in which he postulated the primacy of emotion over cognition. Lazarus (1982, 1984) took the opposite view in stating that there is no emotion without cognition. Arguments for and against these extreme positions are found in the examination of evolutionary or structural factors as well as in the experimental literature. Nevertheless, the question remains open and a credible theory of emotion is awaited.

Meanwhile, Rachman (1980) attempted to integrate clinical and experimental observations in a model of emotional processing. In this model, he proposed a number of factors as likely to facilitate or impede emotional processing. Personal as well as environment factors are implicated in the model. Lang (1978) also proposed a model of emotional processing drawing from investigations of emotional imagery. Rachman (1981) related Zajonc's original analysis of emotion and cognition to the three-component analysis of fear and the desynchrony observed in therapeutic outcome studies carried out earlier when all three systems were measured (Hodgson & Rachman 1974; Rachman & Hodgson 1974). These observations led to the conclusion that these systems (subjective, behavioural and physiological) were loosely coupled and that they were likely to vary in the degree they troubled each and everyone coming for treatment. It was therefore argued that there should be some correspondence between the poorly functioning component and the choice of therapy. Support for this position was discussed in the previous chapter.

The study of physiology as a means of understanding human nature has a great deal of appeal for some people. For one thing, human bodies are tangible. In addition to human observations, experimental manipulations of animals are feasible where ethical considerations would not permit similar manipulations of human beings. It is often thought that such a reductionist approach would contribute to the development of a unified science of human behaviour. An eloquent defence of this position was presented by Gray (1985) at an invited lecture at the 1984 Annual Conference of the British Psychological Society when he was presented with the Presidents' Award of the Society. During the lecture, Gray presented convincing evidence for the use-fulness of research with animals to the understanding of human clinical problems. However, reducing all psycho-logical phenomena to physiology has not been possible, particularly with regard to those phenomena relating to human consciousness. This is not to say that neuro-psychology (a specialization within psychology) has not advanced our understanding by its study of the neuro-chemical, neurophysiological and neurofunctional activities of the brain. It is evident that gross as well as minimal abnormal behaviour can be caused by brain damage and other types of physiological malfunctioning.

The last two chapters have dealt with changing overt behaviour and changing covert behaviour (or those private events experienced in the client's consciousness). The present chapter completes a tripartite perspective on human problematic behaviour by looking at the influence of physiology on abnormal behaviour, the influence of other aspects of behaviour on physiology and current methods used to modify physiological responses.

Physiological problems

Disordered behaviour due to physical trauma and medical illness has long been recognized, such as in cases where mental retardation is clearly attributed to birth injury or certain illnesses of the mother during pregnancy. The specificity of the trauma or physical illness involved in behavioural disorders is linked to the progress of physiology and medicine. A comprehensive review of behavioural disorders associated with central nervous system dysfunction was compiled by Parsons and Hart (1984). However, in another review of biological variables in psychopathology, Fowles (1984) took schizophrenia as a disease entity to illustrate that no adequate and comprehensive theory of psychopathology was possible without taking into account biological and psychological aetiological factors.

Linking psychological factors with physiological problems has also had a long history in psychological writings. The assumption that certain psychological conditions can cause physiological disturbances or damage is held by such disparate groups as psychoanalysts and physiologists. For instance, Breuer and Freud (1893) reported on the case of a little girl who suffered for some years from convulsive attacks which had been diagnosed as epileptic when she was referred to them. During treatment she was hypnotized and, under hypnosis, had one of her attacks. At being questioned regarding what she was seeing, she said that she was seeing a dog coming for her. They were able to establish that the child's first attack could be dated on the day she had been chased by a savage dog. Her behaviour mimicked a physiologically based disorder but was in reality the conversion of her traumatic experience into convulsions. Breuer and Freud claimed that the successful treatment of the girl confirmed their diagnosis of conversion hysteria. In their eyes, the essence of conversion hysteria was that the condition produces symptoms similar to those caused by a physical disorder but without leaving permanent traces.

From a very different perspective, the physiologist Cannon (1942) drew attention to the fact that vital bodily organs could be damaged if the autonomic nervous system was maintained in a highly aroused state through prolonged periods of psychological stress without the opportunity for effective action. Arousal of the autonomic nervous system (ANS) is regarded as a sign of emotion and a natural reaction to aversive or noxious events. It is also transient. However, in a number of disorders widely diagnosed as psychosomatic or psychophysiological, the usually reversible autonomic damage and hormone response to stress is irreversible tissue damage. As a result of several years of experimental work, primarily with animals, Selye (1976) defined stress as the rate of wear and tear caused by life. He conceptualized stress responses as making up a syndrome which he labelled the general adaptation syndrome (GAS), comprising three distinct stages. The first stage is the *alarm reaction*, described as 'the bodily expression of a generalized call to arms of the defensive forces of the organism'. In the second stage, the *stage of resistance*, some degree of adaptation occurs as many of the bodily processes mobilized during the alarm reaction stage work in the opposite direction to ensure survival of the organism. The third stage, the *stage of exhaustion*, is characterized by symptoms similar to those of the first stage.

In sum, physical dysfunction can cause psychological problems and psychological problems can cause physical dysfunction. Before going on to discuss methods of changing physiological responses, it is necessary to look more closely at the so-called psychosomatic or psychophysiological disorders.

Psychosomatic/psychophysiological disorders

Psychosomatic medicine is concerned with the understanding of the part played by psychological factors in physical diseases. It has been extended to include certain psychoneurotic reactions such as conversion hysteria. Alexander (1950) published an influential book entitled *Psychosomatic Medicine*, which stimulated research into the dynamics of psychosomatic manifestations. His own research was directed at finding links between certain unconscious emotional conflict based on psychoanalytical concepts and specific physical disorders. Unfortunately, very little support was obtained for his position due, in part, to the fact that the conflicts proposed lacked definition.

Claridge (1973) noted that the idea of psychosomatic medicine appeared and disappeared in history and traced its recent root to the psychophysiology of emotion. He also tried to bring some order in the area by attempting to classify the types of physical diseases with a potential for psychological involvement into three categories. These diseases, unlike conversion hysteria, involve real damage to the body. The first category included diseases in which the organic pathology is found in the form of a virus or other microorganism. In these diseases psychological factors are not primary. The second category included diseases where exact causes are unknown, for instance, some malignant diseases may have a psychological aetiology. However, this is a very controversial area. The third category included a number of disorders which are often referred to as stress diseases or psychophysiological disorders. Nine psychophysiological disorders were listed in DSM-II. All of these were attributed in part to the emotional state of the patients but differed as to the part of the body which was affected. They included: psychophysiological skin disorders, psychophysiological respiratory disorders, psychophysiological cardiovascular disorders, psychophysiological haemic and lymphatic disorders, psychophysiological gastrointestinal disorders, psychophysiological genital-urinary disorders, psychophysiological endocrine disorders, psychophysiological disorders of a sense organ and psychophysiological musculoskeletal disorders. Claridge's threefold classification of diseases makes it clear that all physical diseases are potentially related to psychological stress and that a revised listing of psychophysiological disorders could become a listing of all diseases. For this reason, DSM-III abandoned psychophysiological disorders in favour of a multi-axial system in which both disease and stressor(s) are identified.

The earliest studies of stress were carried out with animals because of the likely resultant ethical problems if humans were stressed severely enough to produce tissue damage. Ethical problems were circumvented when subjects were studied after naturally occurring disasters or wars but these are relatively infrequent events (Rachman 1978). However, a new methodology was developed by Holmes and Rahe (1967) when they devised the Social Readjustment Rating Scale (SRRS) which was based on a list of 43 discrete social or life events for which high consensus was obtained when subjects were asked to rank them in accordance with their relative degree of necessary readjustment. The items had been chosen in the light of clinical experience; some of them were considered clearly undesirable, such as deaths of loved ones, while others were usually considered desirable, such as vacations or promotion at work, under the assumption that all changes (good or bad) need some degree of readjustment and are therefore stressful. This methodology provided a measure of stress which was shown to be implicated in many physical and psychological disorders (Dohrenwend & Dohrenwend 1974). The methodology is not without its critics (Cleary 1980; Kanner, Coyne, Schaefer & Lazarus 1981), but it nevertheless stimulated a large amount of research into the field. Many clinicians routinely look for such precipitants when evaluating patients presenting with either psychological or physical disorders. For instance, the author would query a new client who was unable to associate specific stress at the time a psychological problem arose regarding the first fourteen or fifteen items at the top of the Social Readjustment Rating Scale. These are in order of magnitude: death of a spouse, divorce, marital separation, jail term, death of a close family member, personal injury or illness, marriage, fired at work, marital reconciliation, retirement, change in health of family member, pregnancy, sex difficulties, gain of a new family member or business readjustment. Often, clients will not have appreciated the degree of experienced stress in these situations and will think of their problems as coming out of a clear blue sky until a careful history reveals some potentially contributing life changes. As an aside, it is interesting to note in Mrs A's history that she had experience of the majority of stressful social readjustment situations listed at the top of the SRRS and that one or other of these had usually preceded a psychological crisis. She recounted the sudden and un-predicted death of a son, personal illness and injury from her husband, marital separation, reconciliation, divorce and, in her recent past, the marriage of her daughters.

Methods of changing physiological responses

Before dealing with behavioural techniques used to change problematic aspects of physiological responding, it is proposed to give examples of palliative measures used to deal with problems emanating from awareness of one's somatic functions. Problems occur when this awareness is heightened, for instance, under strong emotional arousal. However, problems resulting from low arousal awareness can also be encountered, for example, in sexually dys-functional individuals.

Dealing with heightened somatic awareness

Somatic awareness is a private experience and it is impossible to tell whether differences are real or better explained as a function of individual perceptions and expectations. The Symptom Questionnaire of Lehrer and Woolfolk (1982), mentioned in Chapter 2, can be administered to assess the degree of somatic awareness of anxiety. Because it is designed to assess the expression of anxiety in somatic, cognitive and behavioural modalities, it can also be used to determine the relative importance of each modality within the totality of anxiety responding and categorize clients accordingly. The following sixteen items evaluate the somatic modality: (1) my throat gets dry; (2) I have difficulty in swallowing; (3) my heart pounds; (4) my limbs tremble; (5) my stomach hurts; (6) my neck feels tight; (7) I feel dizzy; (8) I breathe rapidly; (9) I can't catch my breath; (10) my arms or legs feel stiff; (11) my muscles twitch or jump; (12) I experience tingling sensation somewhere in my body; (13) my arms or legs feel weak; (14) I experience muscular aches and pains; (15) I feel numbness in my face, limbs, or tongue; (16) I experience chest pains. Respondents are instructed to *circle the number that indicates how he/she feels for each item* on a 0–8 points scale graded from *never* to *extremely often*.

Mrs A obtained high scores on all scales of the Lehrer and Woolfolk Symptom Questionnaire but her score on the somatic scale was proportionally higher than those she obtained on the cognitive and behavioural scales. She had described her feelings in situations she avoided in the following way: 'I feel as if I'm going to pass out. My heart starts pounding' (p. 25). Later she goes on with: 'My mouth gets dry and actually I'm not breathing properly. It is a terrible feeling' (p. 30). She dated the onset of her anxiety problems to puberty: 'At this age it would come to me all of a sudden and I'd just run out of school and run right home gasping for breath'; the result of her behaviour was, 'my grandmother used to take me to the priest and he would bless me and my heart was pounding the whole time' (p. 34). When questioned as to whether she thought she had a heart condition, she replied: 'Oh yes, I was sure of it and I probably still am. I would dwell on my heart and I'd be feeling my pulse. That was the one thing on my mind' (p. 34). At the end of the interview, when given a description of the aims of the therapeutic programme, she commented: 'The part I'm interested in now is what you said about bodily control. Will I remember, when I become panicky? . . . When I get a panic attack I think that, the next time, I won't let it get to me but it still gets to me' (pp. 54–5).

Many but not all agoraphobics claim to experience panic

attacks but no reliable definition of the phenomenon exists. Goldstein and Chambless (1978), in their conceptualization of agoraphobia, viewed 'fear of fear' as the most central phenomenological aspect of the disorder. They further suggested that agoraphobics have a tendency to 'mis-apprehend the causal antecedents of uncomfortable feelings', particularly when an interpersonal conflict is involved. In their words:

> When this interpersonal conflict situation persists long enough or is worsened by other events such as illness or death of a significant other, the preagoraphobic person is likely to experience sharp outbreaks of very high anxiety-panic attacks ... The physical sensations during these panic attacks ... are often interpreted by the client as a sign of impending death by a heart attack or of loss of consciousness (Goldstein & Chambless 1978, A reanalysis of agoraphobia, *Behavior Therapy*: 54).

Physical relaxation techniques. The part played by relaxation training in systematic desensitization was discussed in Chapter 3, as well as the fact that relaxation is acknowledged to produce therapeutic effects on its own. More recently, attempts have been made to test the hypothesis that matching a client's characteristic mode of anxiety responding with appropriate behavioural technique would produce better results than not matching in clients presenting with phobic and anxiety symptoms (Mackay & Liddell 1986; Öst & Hugdahl 1981; Öst, Jerremalm & Jansson 1984; Öst, Johansson & Jerremalm 1982. In the first listed study, clients were divided according to whether they showed anxiety primarily cognitively versus one or other of the other modes. In the remaining three, comparisons of behavioural and physiological responders were carried out. In all four studies, relaxation therapy was given as the treatment of choice for physiological or somatic responders; all studies except the last one listed offered support for the superiority of a physiologically focused technique for somatic responders. In addition, Mackay and Liddell (1986) noted that their somatic responders were generally more anxious than the non-somatic responders, making less progress in treatment than the others. The lack of progress of the somatic responders was particularly evident under the unmatched condition, that is, when they were treated with a cognitive technique. It was suggested that relaxation may be considered as an initial step in the treatment of agoraphobia so that agoraphobics may be helped to bring their physiological responses under some degree of control before being able to reverse avoidance and/or benefit from a cognitive approach. The programme which Mrs A followed was based on this assumption and, while clients were given both relaxation and cognitive therapy, relaxation was introduced first.

Respiratory control treatment. Panic attacks are not always situational but they invariably terrify individuals who experience them as strong physical sensations usually described in one or more of the following ways – palpitations, tachycardia, breathlessness, blurred vision, dizziness, virtigo, nausea, numbness or tingling in the extremities. It is not uncommon for individuals who claim to experience panic attacks to construe these as evidence that they are about to die, have a heart attack, go out of their mind or make a spectacle of themselves. To help individuals who presented with distressing physical sensations of unknown aetiology at a chest clinic, Lum (1976) developed a treatment involving respiratory control. This approach is being developed as a form of relaxation training for overanxious individuals. It is commonly observed in clinical practice that individuals presenting with panic attacks breathe rapidly and shallowly. In the past three years, the author has compared the respiratory rate of clients who reported panic attacks with interns she was training. The interns have usually produced between 13 and 17 breaths per minute while resting but clients showed much higher rates, usually in the 20s or 30s. Both clients and interns could be trained to slow down their breathing to 8 or 9 breaths per minute with resultant feelings of relaxation and calmness. The main assumption behind the initiation of respiratory control techniques was that the symptoms reported were similar to those produced by hyperventilation, suggesting that hyperventilation may play an important role in panic attacks. Clark, Salkovskis and Chalkley (1985) carried out an evaluation of a respiratory control programme which included a number of components. Prior to training in respiratory control, clients were asked to 'breathe quickly and deeply through their mouth' for approximately two minutes. Following overbreathing, clients were asked to fill in Clark and Hemsley's (1982) symptoms rating sheet as a way of monitoring their sensations as well as to make rating of the comparability of the effects of overbreathing and their panic attacks; only individuals who perceived marked similarity between the sensations of panic and those of hyperventilation were included in the study. These clients were given an explanation of how hyperventilation induces panic and training in slowing down their breathing. Slow breathing was practised with the aid of a pacing tape until clients were able to start slow regular breathing without prompting from the tape. Once respiratory control was achieved, clients were asked to hyperventilate for a few seconds, then work at controlling the resultant sensations by switching to the slow, relaxed pattern of breathing they had perfected. After completion of the programme, clients showed a significant reduction in panic attacks as well as decreases in a number of distress self-ratings. The technique proved beneficial to clients who had situational fears as well as those who could not identify situations which consistently aroused anxiety.

Like other relaxation techniques, respiratory control training has been carried out in different ways, making comparisons of outcome studies difficult. It is evident that many therapists have drawn their procedures from the meditation techniques of the East. Bacon and Poppen (1985) attempted to bring some order by defining respiratory manoeuvres derived from Eastern meditative techniques. They isolated five such manoeuvres:

1. Diaphragmatic breathing, in which the abdomen rises and falls while the upper chest remains relatively still.
2. Nasal breathing, in which air is inhaled and exhaled through the nose rather than the mouth.
3. Regular breathing, in which the rate and extent of breathing cycles is consistent over time.
4. Slow breathing, in which the frequency is decreased from the normal rate of breathing.
5. Focus on breathing, in which the person is instructed, or instruct him/herself, to concentrate on certain aspects of breathing (Bacon & Poppen 1985, A behavioral analysis of diaphramatic breathing and its effects on peripheral temperature, *Journal of Behavior Therapy and Experimental Psychiatry*: 16).

Respiratory control training programmes have been based on one or more of these techniques but we are not in a position to comment on their relative efficacy.

Dealing with low arousal

Modern systems for the classification of sexual disorders were initially based on behavioural criteria. These were undoubtedly influenced by the pioneering work of Masters and Johnson (1970), whose direct observations of the human sexual response cycle and the ensuing treatment of dysfunctional responses revolutionized our thinking. However, as was noted in a recent review (Friedman, Weiler, LoPiccolo & Hogan 1982), uncomplicated sexual problems are becoming a rarity in clinical practice. They concluded that the plethera of widely available self-help books and the dissemination of relevant information in the public press have left the clinician with more complicated cases involving individual pathology, severe marital distress and, increasingly, clients who bring complaints of low desire and aversion to sex.

Sexual growth programmes. As early as 1972 Lobitz and LoPiccolo reported on a nine-step programme for inorgasmic women. The programme involved a series of logically graded steps in which inorgasmic women were encouraged to begin with a visual examination of their genitals with a mirror, followed by tactile exploration to locate then stimulate *pleasure-sensitive* areas, experimenting with erotic fantasies, explicitly erotic visual material or vibrators depending on preference and need. The programme was elaborated in a widely used self-help book entitled *Becoming Orgasmic: Sexual Growth Program for Women* (Heiman, LoPiccolo and LoPiccolo 1976). The authors approached sexual growth as an instance of personal growth in which 'change comes from exploring new ways to think and feel as well as new things to do with your body' (Heiman, LoPiccolo & LoPiccolo 1976, *Becoming Orgasmic*, Prentice Hall: 6).

Monitoring physiological reactions for change

In many cases, the taking of psychophysiological measures is involved in treatment. This is particularly true when biofeedback is used as a therapeutic tool. Biofeedback training is based on the close monitoring of some autonomic bodily function, for example, muscle tension, heart rate, blood pressure, skin conductance, skin temperature, brain wave. The physiological process targeted for retraining is detected and amplified by sensitive electronic equipment which amplifies the signal detected to give immediate and accurate information on internal physiological functioning auditorily or visually. In this way, clients are made aware of physiological responses they have little means of being aware of, so that they can work at modifying them. To illustrate the wide range of methods in use for the modification of physiological responses, examples of techniques used in the treatment of headaches and Raynaud's disease will follow.

Headaches. Headaches are acknowledged as a common complaint often not brought beyond the general practitioner (Leviton 1978; Philips 1977; Turner & Stone 1979). The classification suggested by the Ad Hoc Committee on the Classification of Headaches (1962) was used widely for diagnosis and research purposes. In this classification system, the two main types of headaches are the muscle contraction or tension headache and the vascular or migraine headache. The classification was based on the assumption that the muscle contraction or tension headache is the result of sustained contraction of muscles in the face, scalp and neck while the migraine or vascular headache was attributed to excessive responding in the form of vaso-constriction or vasodilation of the cranial or cerebral arteries. However, some individuals report both types of headache.

Budzinski, Stoyva and Adler (1970) developed an instru-mental procedure by which tension headache sufferers were given feedback on the electromyographic (EMG) activity levels of their frontalis muscles while learning to relax them. This was viewed as incorporating two major characteristics of operant conditioning, namely, immediate knowledge of results and the gradual shaping of appropriate responses. Clients undergoing this form of treatment were asked to keep daily records of the frequency and intensity of their headaches and outcome was based on these. The authors reported that the period of time needed for improvement varied from client to client between four weeks and two months. The five clients they included in this initial study learned to lower frontalis EMG levels and reported fewer headaches. The procedure was subsequently used and investigated widely. The method has not been without its critics on the grounds that not all tension headache sufferers show raised EMG activity or respond as well to biofeedback training (Philips & Hunter 1981a, 1981b).

Peripheral temperature training was first developed by Sargent, Walters and Green (1973), when it was observed by them that a subject who was participating in a study investigating the effects of temperature feedback on hand-warming was able to prevent a migranous attack by raising the temperature of the hand. The ensuing temperature training programme involved giving migraine sufferers differential temperature feedback to train them to raise the temperature of their hands relative to the temperature of their forehead. They combined this form of biofeedback training with autogenic training, a relaxation therapy developed by Schultz and Luthe (1969).

In a comprehensive review of psychological assessment and treatment of headaches, Blanchard and Andrasik (1982) concluded that biofeedback alone, relaxation alone and biofeedback and relaxation together were shown equally efficacious in decreasing tension headaches. A later replication study of 250 chronic headache patients concluded that 41 per cent of tension headache patients responded to relaxation alone, while 52 per cent of migraine and combined headache patients improved with a combination of relaxation and thermal biofeedback (Blanchard, Andrasik, Evans, Neff, Appelbaum & Rodichok 1985).

Raynaud's disease. The symptoms of Raynaud's disease are thought to be secondary to extreme vasodilation of the blood vessels of the hands and feet. Patients who experience these vasospatic attacks in the hands and/or feet also experience a great deal of pain. Attacks are known to be precipitated by cold temperature and emotional stress. Since the 1970s two types of biofeedback procedures are used to treat the disorder. The first involves direct training in peripheral vasodilation, and the other, hand-warming. Jobe, Sampson, Roberts and Kelly (1986) reviewed the types of behavioural treatments given for Raynaud's disease in an introduction to a study comparing classical conditioning therapy with biofeedback plus relaxation. They found no difference between the methods at the end of training but, after one year follow-up, classical conditioning was found to be more effective.

In summary, it can be said that the possibilities for the development of biofeedback training are numerous and dependent on the identification and monitoring of an appropriate faulty bodily response known to cause pathology. A note of caution is nevertheless necessary at this stage. It was clear in the above examples that there were alternative effective methods of treatment to biofeedback, in particular, various forms of relaxation therapy which are much less costly and which are thought more likely to increase patients' perception of self-control. It is also true that most people's homeostatic bodily mechanisms work naturally and need no training. Therefore, individuals who receive biofeedback training may not always be able to make the expected switch to self-control without external prompting.

Chapter 6

Inoculation and prevention

The initial success of behaviour therapy based on systematic desensitization and related approaches, gave rise to an expansion of techniques and types of clients on whom they were applied. Within this context, 'coping' strategies to help clients achieve control over a host of maladaptive responses were gradually developed. This necessitated a change of paradigm in which control was shifted from therapist to patient. It also offered possibilities for greater generalization and prevention. Traditional behavioural interventions were primarily based on a mastery model, which assumed that therapeutic success was achieved once the therapist had helped his/her client towards recovery measured as the elimination of (or mastery over) discrete, situation-specific responses. A need was felt for procedures to give clients coping skills applicable across situations and problems.

Psychoanalysis had predicted that tackling symptoms directly would lead to symptom substitution but this did not seem to happen to clients who had been treated symptomatically by behaviour therapists (Yates 1958). However, clients who presented with more complex problems than well-circumscribed phobias took longer to desensitize and were more likely to bring new problems to their therapists. Kazdin (1982b) recently reassessed issues relating to symptom substitution and generalization. He saw four types of difficulties to be serious deterrents to the scientific study of symptom substitution. The first is the difficulty of identifying symptoms as separate from underlying disorders; the second, the difficulty of establishing a connection between the original and substitute symptom; the third comes from the lack of specificity regarding the time frame for substitution, since substitution could just as well occur any time after treatment as several years hence. The fourth difficulty involves determining whether a new symptom emerging after treatment is a substitute brought on by treatment, a new problem in its own right or, alternatively, a symptom which was present before treatment but over-shadowed by the main problem treated. He concluded that the ideas surrounding symptom substitution had been instrumental in stimulating more debate than empirical research and offered his own conceptualization of the phenomenon based on response covariation. He viewed response in the widest sense of the word to mean

> the full range of dependent measures that are of potential
> interest in a particular person's behavior. Thus, responses
> encompass data obtained through different assessment methods
> such as self-report, projective techniques, observations of overt
> behavior, psychophysiological methods, and others. Also,
> responses would include affect, cognitions, overt behavior, and
> other levels of measuring personality and behavior (Kazdin
> 1982b, Symptom substitution, generalization, and response
> covariation, *Psychological Bulletin*: 352).

It follows from learning principles that, when two or more responses are similar or share common characteristics, change in one of them affects other responses – they are said to covary. Taken in the context of behaviour therapy, it is evident that changes may occur in untreated responses due to this relationship. It is also understood that changes may be both positive and negative. Response covariation was offered as an alternative concept to replace both symptom substitution and generalization. Kazdin (1982b) found support for his arguments in a number of reports from the behaviour therapy literature.

Inoculation techniques

Three approaches which emphasize training of clients in the acquisition of coping strategies to achieve some degree of control over non-target behaviours or non-target situations will be discussed. These include training in anxiety management, self-control and stress inoculation. The first two approaches derive more directly from conditioning principles than the last one, which is a more cognitively based method than the other two.

Anxiety management training (AMT)

Suinn and Richardson (1971) developed their AMT programme in response to the limitations inherent in systematic desensitization. It was always evident that systematic desensitization was not designed to prepare clients for coping with tensions encountered after treatment. In addition, not all clients can imagine fear stimuli well enough to benefit from SD. Furthermore, SD looked less appealing as a treatment for people whose problems involved generalized anxiety, due to the time and energy needed to organize a hierarchy representing several categories of aversive stimuli as well as for the number of exposure sessions necessary to move systematically up such lengthy hierarchies. It is also true that many individuals who present with anxiety problems experience free-floating anxiety, that is, are unable to identify external cues for their excessive anxiety responses.

To expand the applicability of behaviour therapy to anxiety based disorders, Suinn and Richardson (1971) decided to work on changing the anxiety response rather than the S-R connections. Theoretically, AMT relies on conditioning principles but it views anxiety as a discriminative stimulus to which clients respond. In other words, internal bodily states associated with the experience of anxiety, such as musculo-skeletal or autonomic responses, can be acquired through conditioning of external stimuli and, in turn, take on cue properties of their own. AMT is directed toward having clients respond with relaxation or competency (success) to the stimulus dimensions of onset or increasing levels of anxiety, unlike SD which attempts to attach the anxiety-provoking stimulus to the relaxation response. It was hoped that this type of training would enable trained individuals to manage anxiety no matter what prompted it.

AMT proceeds in three stages. The first stage involves the therapist giving the client a rationale for the procedure, followed by deep muscular relaxation training. The second stage is concerned with training in visualizing scenes arousing anxiety interspersed with scenes associated with relaxation and competency. During this stage, therapists encourage their clients to attend to anxiety response cues. Practice in switching from scene to scene leads to the final stage, which aims at giving the client experience at anxiety arousal and anxiety control. To reduce therapy time, massed presentations over several hours rather than spaced sessions were introduced. While there are obvious similarities between AMT and systematic desensitization and also flooding, there are also important differences. In addition to shortening therapy time and giving clients resources to cope independently with life stresses, it is also thought to produce less discomfort in the individual treated in this way because he/she is not continuously faced with anxiety experiences but learns to switch from anxiety experiences to relaxation or competency. The programme was originally tested with students presenting with mathematics anxiety (Richardson & Suinn 1973). In a more recent version of the programme, Suinn (1981) attests to its usefulness for clients:

> diagnosed as generalized anxiety disorder, as well as with persons with less debilitating general anxiety, with schizophrenics, Type A persons, and delinquents ... The AMT model has been applied also to treatment of tension headaches, high blood pressure, and persons with performance or with test anxiety. Although AMT has been used with phobics, desensitization is probably a more appropriate method for single phobias while AMT is more efficient with multiple

phobias (Suinn 1981, *Manual Anxiety Management Training*, Rocky Mountain Behavioral Sciences Institute: 1).

Self-control training

Self-control training is most clearly contrasted with the passive conditioning process postulated for systematic desensitization. For instance, clients who have undergone SD of a particular fear expect that the counterconditioning process will have reduced that fear without the need to do anything further. Kanfer (1980) contrasted an *administrative* therapy model as being the traditional one underlying the activities of the majority of mental health professionals, with a *participant* model emphasizing the importance of client responsibility in treatment. Skinner (1953) had set the scene for the implementation of self-control procedures almost twenty years before they were actually developed. The time-lag occurred because of reluctance on the part of other behaviourists to introduce what had been rejected as unverifiable mentalistic concepts. Self-control was too closely linked to hazy constructs such as willpower. However, Skinner's conceptual analysis of *self-control* was made in operant terms and went thus:

> The individual often comes to control part of his own behavior when a response has conflicting consequences – when it leads to both positive and negative reinforcement. Drinking alcoholic beverages, for example, is often followed by a condition of unusual confidence in which one is more successful socially and in which one forgets responsibilities, anxieties, and other troubles. Since this is positively reinforcing, it increases the likelihood that drinking will take place on future occasions. But there are other consequences – the physical illness of the 'hang-over' and the possibly disastrous effects of over-confident or irresponsible behavior – which are negatively reinforcing and, when contingent upon behavior, represent a form of punishment. If punishment were simply the reverse of reinforcement, the two might combine to produce an intermediate tendency to drink, but we have seen that this is not the case. When a similar occasion arises, the same or an increased tendency to drink will prevail; but the occasion as

well as the early stages of drinking will generate conditioned aversive stimuli and emotional responses to them which we speak of as shame or guilt. The emotional responses may have some deterrent effect in weakening behavior – as by 'spoiling the mood'. A more important effect, however, is that any behavior which weakens the behavior of drinking is automatically reinforced by the resulting reduction in aversive stimulation. We have discussed the behavior of simply 'doing something else', which is reinforced because it displaces punishable behavior, but there are other possibilities. The organism may make the punished response less probable by altering the variables of which it is a function. Any behavior which succeeds in doing this will automatically be reinforced. We call such behavior self-control (Skinner 1953, *Science and Human Behavior*, Free Press: 230).

Kanfer and Philips (1970) classified self-control problems into two categories. The first category includes types of behaviour which are self-defeating or injurious, such as substance abuse or smoking and various forms of antisocial behaviour. In such cases, therapists help clients reduce the occurrence of the behaviour. In the second category, therapists need to help and encourage their clients to engage in infrequent but desirable behaviour such as initiating social contact, sexual activity, work or study. It is thought that, at least in principle, self-control procedures can be applied to any behavioural problem providing the client has sufficient intelligence to understand and carry out such a programme (Rimm & Masters 1979).

Mahoney and Thoresen (1974), in a widely read book of the period entitled *Self-Control: Power to the Person*, listed three basic elements necessary to the training of human self-control: (1) awareness of controlling influence; (2) environmental changes that encourage the desired outcome; and (3) self-presented consequences. Awareness is achieved by asking clients to carry out systematic self-observations and keeping records of these observations for the purpose of feedback and evaluation. It was mentioned earlier (Ch. 2) that the monitoring of desired behaviour can often have a positive effect (reactivity). However, the effect of monitoring undesirable behaviour is not so clear-cut. There are several ways of monitoring behaviour depending on the behaviour in question and whether it is frequent or infrequent, but it is crucial to note the circumstances in which the behaviour occurs such as antecedents, the environment (including people present) and consequences. In other words, clients are taught to make functional analyses (like those described in Ch. 2) of their own behaviour as the first step in training for self-control. Often the recording is done in the form of a daily diary. With behaviour which has very high frequency of occurrence, such as smoking or obsessive thinking, the use of mechanical counters has been found helpful. The literature is replete with suggestions for recording various forms of behaviour reliably and meaningfully (Clay 1983; Farrell 1986). Once a behavioural analysis is carried out, environmental planning is put into operation as a method of effecting change. In practice, this means that changes will be engineered in either the cues which precede the response to be changed or in its consequences.

A good example of self-control training is that involved in the behavioural treatment of obesity. Obese individuals are easy to detect and several aspects of the problem lend themselves to good measurement. Body weight or skinfold thickness are objective outcome measures and the calorific value of food with consideration of the expension of energy through various activities are appropriate measurable units on which to base dietary changes. The obese client is trained to appreciate the importance of stimulus control while self-monitoring, such as the importance of *how, where, when, with whom* or the *what* consumed. Stunkard (1984) proposed a threefold classification of obesity based on percent of 'overweightness' compared with ideal or average weights – mild (20–40 per cent), moderate (41–100 per cent) and severe (100+ per cent). On the basis of information available in the literature, White (1986) suggested a different treatment approach for children and adolescents fitting into each of the three different Stunkard categories. With mild obesity, she advocated a preventive approach emphasizing long-term changes in both eating and activity patterns with the canvassing of parental support. On the other hand, more comprehensive behavioural programmes were deemed necessary for the other two categories, with extended treatment periods, increased frequency of client-therapist contact, direct parental involvement, deposit-refund contracts and, in certain cases, radical dietary interventions conducted in hospitals for the severely overweight youngsters. It is clear that the development of self-control regarding healthy eating and activity patterns needs to be tackled differently depending on the severity of the problem and that the efficacy of a treatment programme will be a function of having achieved the right kind of balance between internal and external control. In a recent overview of work carried out with obese children, Hart (1986) concluded that, in general, behavioural weight management procedures were found to be effective but adherence after termination of formal programmes was a problem; therefore we needed to sharpen our ability to teach self-control in that area.

Stress inoculation training (SIT)

Meichenbaum's Stress Inoculation Training was designed to reduce and prevent maladaptive stress reactions (Meichenbaum 1977, 1985). Stress is viewed by the author

> as neither a stimulus nor a response, but rather as the result of a 'transaction', influenced by both the individual and the environment. From a transactional perspective, stress is defined as a cognitively mediated relational concept. It reflects the relationship between the person and the environment that is appraised by the person as taxing or exceeding his or her resources and as endangering his or her well-being
> (Meichenbaum 1985, *Stress Inoculation Training*, Pergamon: 3).

The transactional nature of stress thus proposed emphasizes the cognitive interpersonal context of stress. Within this approach to behaviour change, the therapist is viewed as a 'trainer' whose function is 'to educate clients about the nature and impact of stress and to ensure that they have the variety of intrapersonal and interpersonal skills to use stress constructively (Meichenbaum 1985: 6).

Cognition is understood as having three aspects: (1) cognitive events referring to conscious, identifiable thoughts and images; (2) cognitive processes or ways in which information is processed to shape mental representation and schemata; (3) cognitive structures taking in beliefs, commitments, and meanings which determine one's construction of the world. SIT trainers involve their clients in looking for connections between these three aspects of cognition and their stress reactions before developing appropriate coping strategies. It is stressed that SIT is not conceptualized as a single technique. On the contrary,

> it is a generic term referring to a treatment paradigm consisting of a semistructured, clinically sensitive training regimen. The specific training operations conducted during the course of training vary, depending upon the population treated. SIT combines elements of didactic teaching, Socratic discussion, cognitive restructuring, problem solving and relaxation training, behavioral and imaginal rehearsal, self-monitoring, self-instruction and self-reinforcement, and efforts at environmental change. SIT is designed to nurture and develop coping skills, not only to resolve specific immediate problems but also to apply to future difficulties. It provides individuals and groups with a proactive defense or a set of coping skills to deal with future stressful situations (Meichenbaum 1985: 21).

It is obvious from the above that a SIT trainer will use many techniques to improve coping styles depending on both client characteristics and their circumstances. A difference is made between coping techniques called instrumental (problem-focused) and palliative (emotional-regulation) after Lazarus and Laurier (1978). Meichenbaum (1985) gave as examples of instrumental coping techniques information gathering, problem solving, communication and social skills training, time management, life-style changes such as reassessing priorities, mobilizing supports, and direct action efforts designed to change the environmental demands or alter stressful situations and transactions. Examples of palliative coping included techniques which 'relieve distress and foster emotion-regulation' such as taking perspective by engaging in social comparisons and searching for meaning, diverting attention, denial, expressing affect, and training in relaxation. The following seven operationally defined practical steps best summarize the SIT approach:

1. Teach clients the transactional nature of stress and coping.
2. Train clients to self-monitor maladaptive thought, images, feelings, and behaviours in order to facilitate adaptive appraisals.
3. Train clients in problem solving, that is, problem definition, consequence, anticipation, decision making, and feedback evaluation.
4. Model and rehearse direct-action, emotion-regulation, and self-control coping skills.
5. Teach clients how to use maladaptive responses as cues to implement their coping repertoires.
6. Offer practice in *in vitro* imaginal and in behavioural rehearsal and in *in vivo* graded assignments that become increasingly demanding to nurture clients' confidence in and utilization of their coping repertoires.
7. Help clients acquire sufficient knowledge, self-understanding and coping skills to facilitate better ways of handling (un)expected stressful situations (Meichenbaum 1985: 22).

It should be added that an integral part of SIT is the notion of *inoculation for failure*. This means that clients are prepared for the possibility of setbacks and lapses. Clients are encouraged to identify high-risk situations and to explore effective coping strategies which will enable the re-establishment of control rather than dwell over feelings of helplessness. SIT has been found applicable to a variety of problems, including problems with anger, performance anxiety, problems with circumscribed fears, general stress reactions, medical problems, health-related problems, victim populations, as well as professional groups who need to deal regularly with stressful situations such as nurses, teachers, police officers, probation officers, parachutists and scuba divers (Meichenbaum 1985).

Mrs A's programme

As already mentioned in Chapter 3, the programme was run as an educational package whereby emphasis was placed on the understanding of anxiety as comprising a loose coupling of three systems (Lang 1969; Rachman 1978) and the relationship between the model and the coping strategies taught – relaxation, thought stopping/restructuring and the selection of realistic and practical goals to overcome avoidance. Clients who agreed to follow the programme were asked to contract with the therapist verbally to come for five consecutive weekly meetings of approximately two hours each, followed by five more weeks of individual work on which they were to report at a further group meeting (week 11) and, again, after six more months. Contracting has been widely used by behaviour therapists to encourage adherence, as when clients put in a deposit at the beginning of a structured programme to be returned if all sessions are attended. An example of this approach was mentioned earlier regarding the treatment of obesity (White 1986). However, more formal written contracts have been used with people who bring interpersonal problems, for example in marital, family or work contexts. One of the main reasons for such contracts is to enable each of the persons involved to communicate his/her own expectations and understand the expectations of others (DeRisi & Butz 1975; Stuart 1980). With the agoraphobic group programme Mrs A agreed to join, it was thought sufficient to have an unwritten agreement, placing trust between therapist and client above all other considerations.

During the first group session, clients were given the

rationale for the programme along with a psychological conceptualization of agoraphobia. Each client had been given a briefing during the initial interview but it was felt that the subject needed to be elaborated at some length before it could be fully understood. It was stressed that the aim of the programme was to prepare them during the first five sessions to become their own therapist by continuing to apply the programme on their own for as long as was required to achieve the goals set. They were told that, following the five weeks of intense work assisted by their therapists, they would be sent for a trial period of five more weeks on their own, then report on their progress during a further group session when any problems encountered would be discussed and, hopefully, ironed out. The role of the therapist was presented as one in which he/she would provide training in anxiety management skills and help clients design a realistic self-paced exposure programme based on individualized hierarchies of items which clients had been avoiding but wished to be comfortable with. It was emphasized that the therapists were consultants who would provide assistance to their clients so that they could get back the control they wished over their behaviour. Clients were randomly assigned to a therapist who had a maximum of three clients to train during each group session. During each session, small group work and large group work alternated according to training needs. The group leader did not have special client responsibility but assisted any therapists who requested it. Certain aspects of the programme will be focused on to give a better understanding of the components aimed specifically at the development of client self-control. These components included steps to foster a clear understanding of the conceptual issues relevant to the programme, monitoring and feedback, choice of coping techniques, use of reinforcement and inoculation.

Conceptualization. The understanding of the treatment paradigm was presented as being a crucial part of the programme. To ensure this, an assessment of individual client's understanding was carried out by means of a test before the start of the programme. Items for the test were taken from the *Client's Manual* provided by Mathews, Gelder and Johnston (1981), Guilford (Table 6.1). Over the years the programme has been in operation, few clients have scored above 50 per cent before the start of the treatment; Mrs A scored well below 50 per cent. Clients were given the manual during the second session and asked to study it carefully and to discuss any part they did not understand with their therapist. They were informed that they would be tested again during Session 4. It was explained to them that the understanding given in the manual was the basis on which their programme would be tailored and implemented and that the test would help them master the information necessary to become their own therapist. In the second testing few clients scored less than 80 per cent. Feedback was given immediately after the test was completed and errors were discussed and corrected individually. At the end of the programme, clients were asked to rank the following aspects of the programme in the order in which they had benefited them – relaxation training, looking for, stopping or changing negative thinking or the booklet (*Client's Manual*) with the explanation and advice regarding agoraphobia. The majority of clients found the *Client's Manual* to be the most helpful of the three components listed.

Monitoring and feedback. Several measures were taken during treatment to evaluate and improve the programme. The principles and practicalities of evaluating a therapy programme will be discussed in the next chapter. However, some of these measures were also used to give clients feedback on their progress. The manner in which goals were chosen from the hierarchy was shown in Chapter 3 with typical homework instructions. The layout of the goal sheet is illustrated in Table 6.2. Each group session after the first one started with a close examination of the goal sheet filled in during the previous week before new goals were set. Another measure of progress was based on the hierarchy which was

Table 6.1 Test of model of agoraphobia and of its treatment

Agoraphobia

Instructions

For each of the questions below, indicate your answer by placing an X in the appropriate place. (.X.)

1. Someone with Agoraphobia is likely to be afraid of:

    (a) Open spaces in the country   (...)
    (b) Losing control in crowded public places   (...)
    (c) Staying at home with someone   (...)
    (d) Being with other people   (...)

2. Agoraphobia panic is different from ordinary fear or shock because:

    (a) It can't be controlled very easily   (...)
    (b) It causes bodily changes, such as your heart's beating
         faster   (...)
    (c) It is an automatic bodily reaction   (...)
    (d) It is the same as fear but without any real danger (...)

3. Conditioning means:

    (a) Association of a reaction with a situation   (...)
    (b) Learning to be afraid   (...)
    (c) An oversensitive state following an illness   (...)
    (d) Learning that two things always go together   (...)

4. If a child has been frightened by a large, fierce dog, would it be best to:

    (a) Keep him/her away from dogs for a while   (...)
    (b) Tell him/her to be braver next time   (...)
    (c) Give him/her candy to cheer him/her up   (...)
    (d) Introduce him/her to a more gentle dog   (...)

5. Agoraphobia is:

    (a) A mental disease such as schizophrenia   (...)
    (b) Due to physical illness   (...)
    (c) A learned emotional reaction   (...)
    (d) Caused by a lack of willpower   (...)

6. If you avoid a store where you had a panic attack:

    (a) You will find it more and more difficult to go back (...)
    (b) In time you will be able to go back without trouble (...)
    (c) You should wait until you are well before going back (...)
    (d) You should get someone else to go into the store for you (...)

Table 6.1 continued

7. Agoraphobic symptoms often include:

    (a) Acting insanely   (...)
    (b) Feeling faint or strange   (...)
    (c) Collapse through physical overstrain   (...)
    (d) No special feelings   (...)

8. If you succeed in going to a particular place that you have avoided for some time:

    (a) It won't give you any more trouble   (...)
    (b) It will be even more difficult the next time   (...)
    (c) It won't have made any difference one way or the other   (...)
    (d) It will probably be slightly easier the next time   (...)

9. Before facing a situation that you have avoided for a long time you should:

    (a) Always take a tranquilizer   (...)
    (b) Avoid taking a tranquilizer if possible; take it only when you have to practise something new or difficult   (...)
    (c) Avoid tranquilizers completely   (...)
    (d) Take a tranquilizer if you feel panicky when going out   (...)

10. Which would be the wrong thing to recommend for someone with agoraphobia:

    (a) Doing things one step at a time   (...)
    (b) Taking tranquilizers before occasional practice sessions   (...)
    (c) Practising going out every day   (...)
    (d) Having help from others with things like shopping   (...)

11. Which of the following would be a useful description of a treatment target:

    (a) Go out for a walk   (...)
    (b) Practise going out every day   (...)
    (c) Walk alone to the school   (...)
    (d) Try to keep calm when shopping in the supermarket   (...)

12. Which of the following would be the best target for an agoraphobic person:

    (a) Start practice in going shopping   (...)
    (b) Go to the local supermarket alone on a Wednesday morning, when it is least crowded   (...)
    (c) Find ways to make yourself feel differently about crowded stores   (...)
    (d) None of these   (...)

Table 6.1 continued

13. Daily practice in learning to overcome avoidance is important because:

  (a) If several days go by without practice, it may get harder   (...)
  (b) It builds confidence for harder items later   (...)
  (c) With each practice, the fear will tend to get less   (...)
  (d) All of these   (...)

14. If you succeed the first time you practise an item, you should:

  (a) Try it again tomorrow   (...)
  (b) Try a more difficult one   (...)
  (c) Try an easier one   (...)
  (d) Congratulate yourself and have a well-earned rest   (...)

15. Which might bridge the gap between 'Walking to the supermarket' and 'Going alone by bus to the school':

  (a) Going with someone by bus to the school   (...)
  (b) Going alone for just one stop at first   (...)
  (c) Going alone, and being met at the other end   (...)
  (d) All of these   (...)

16. Practice items between target behaviours are useful because:

  (a) They are slightly easier than the last target item successfully practised   (...)
  (b) They build confidence   (...)
  (c) They bridge any large gaps in difficulty between targets   (...)
  (d) All of these   (...)

17. Suppose you succeed with practice after taking several pills but then find that you cannot manage without any. You should:

  (a) Go on to the next most difficult item   (...)
  (b) Repeat the same item several times   (...)
  (c) Stop practice for a while   (...)
  (d) Gradually reduce the dose while practising the same item   (...)

18. Which is a correct description of treatment practice:

  (a) Try each item once; if successful, move on   (...)
  (b) Decide on target behaviours, and practise one every day   (...)
  (c) Start practising with easier items, and progress to more difficult ones   (...)
  (d) Use tranquilizers during all treatment practice sessions   (...)

Table 6.1 continued

19. Which of these is likely to cause or contribute to a panic attack:

    (a) The conditioned fear reaction to certain places (...)
    (b) Worry about strange feelings during practice (...)
    (c) Thinking that the fear is going to get out of control (...)
    (d) All of these (...)

20. Which would you say indicates most progress:

    (a) Doing something new without any trouble the first time (...)
    (b) Trying something new even if you have to come back because of tension (...)
    (c) Doing something new despite experiencing some panic at first (...)
    (d) Doing something new but finishing in a total panic (...)

21. If you become frightened in a store, it would be best to:

    (a) Try to snap out of it (...)
    (b) Get home as soon as possible (...)
    (c) Go to another store (...)
    (d) Stay until you feel better (...)

22. You are on a bus. In a panic, you find yourself getting off earlier than planned. You should:

    (a) Force yourself to get on the next bus (...)
    (b) Try again, soon, possibly after taking a tranquilizer (...)
    (c) Try an easier 'in-between' item (...)
    (d) All of these (...)

23. The best way to cope with panic during practice is to:

    (a) Continue practice without stopping (...)
    (b) Let it happen and wait for it to pass (...)
    (c) Go home and relax (...)
    (d) Take a tranquilizer as soon as possible (...)

24. A job or outside interest is important because:

    (a) It provides regular practice in going out (...)
    (b) It is a source of satisfaction away from home (...)
    (c) Meeting new situations and people helps break the habit of avoidance (...)
    (d) All of these (...)

Table 6.2 Goal sheet

NAME...

DATE ....

GOAL(S)

	How often	*How long*

....

....

....

....

....

....

....

....

transferred on a separate sheet to carry out a microanalysis
of self-efficacy in relation to each one of the items on the
hierarchy (Bandura 1977). The form used for this purpose
was adapted from one illustrated in Barlow's 1981 book
Behavioral Assessment of Adult Disorders (see Table 7.1,
p. 152). Thirty lines were drawn on the form and the
hierarchy items were listed on every second line to encourage
clients to consider sub-goals when they found themselves

unable to progress beyond a certain point. Clients were repeatedly told that failures could often be attributed to having moved up the hierarchy too quickly. A microanalysis of each hierarchy item was taken weekly after the first week so that clients could appreciate for themselves changes in performance as well as in confidence levels. Another weekly measure introduced was that of monitoring their levels of anxiety four times a day (Table 6.3). This was used to attempt to locate stressful times and discuss ways of dealing with any identified stressful situation in an effective way. It was also used to show that clients were affected by what was going on around them, contrary to a belief shared by many agoraphobics that anxiety comes out of a clear blue sky making it dangerous and uncontrollable.

Coping techniques. The rationale for the use of relaxation and thought stopping/restructuring was discussed in Chapters 3, 4 and 5. Suffice to add at this stage that clients were encouraged to try all the techniques they were taught and to choose from experience those which helped them most. The use of any other idiosyncratic but successful strategy was also encouraged. One client could not relax but saw the necessity for a relaxing time in her busy and stressful life. She had found running very beneficial some years previously and decided with her therapist's encouragement to start it up again. This worked splendidly for her again and she was also able to tolerate more arousal due to anxiety as a result of it. Physiological arousal stopped being identified exclusively with anxiety feelings in her mind.

Reinforcement and inoculation. Many individual discussions throughout the programme centred on reinforcement and inoculation, particularly at the end of the therapist-assisted phase of the programme. The focus of the fifth session was a discussion of the self-designed programme each client had brought to his/her therapist for revision. Therapists made sure that each programme involved appropriate reinforcement and much was made of the

Table 6.3   Measure of background level of anxiety

ANXIETY SCALE

Please choose a number from the scale below to show how anxious you are during the *days* and *times* listed.

0	1	2	3	4	5	6	7	8
Hardly at all		Slightly anxious		Definitely anxious		Markedly anxious		Very anxious

	Getting up	Before lunch	Before dinner	Going to bed
Thursday				
Friday				
Saturday				
Sunday				
Monday				
Tuesday				
Wednesday				

Name . . . .

Date . . . .

vagaries of human nature and the necessity to learn to tolerate lapses and failures as problems to be solved rather than disasters.

Chapter 7

Evaluation of the efficacy of methods of changing behaviour

For the past thirty-five years or so, evaluating the efficacy of psychotherapy has remained one of the biggest challenges for researchers in the field. It is obviously important to know which methods produce the best results and with whom but it is equally important to know why, to be able to improve on existing procedures. An indication of the degree of continuing interest in psychotherapy research is the simultaneous publication of two recent numbers of well-respected psychology periodicals entirely devoted to psychotherapy research. In February 1986 the editors of the *American Psychologist* and of the *Journal of Consulting and Clinical Psychology* gathered together authors belonging to different schools of psychotherapy in an effort to present their readers with the state of the art (and hopefully science) of psychotherapy. VandenBos (1986) introduced the special issue of the *American Psychologist* by stating that a consensus of sorts had been reached that 'psychotherapy, as a generic process, was demonstrably more effective than no treatment'. In the same issue, Stiles, Shapiro and Elliott (1986) concluded that all psychotherapies are probably drawing from a 'common pool of psychological change'. The pressing problem is undoubtedly related to the discovery of the key processes determining therapeutic changes. Before discussing the status of behaviour therapy, it is intended to discuss some general methodological issues.

Methodological issues

The methodology used to test the relative efficacy of various drug treatments has greatly influenced the design of studies assessing the effects of therapy. As an example, let us go through the steps that are likely to be taken by a fictitious research team who are organizing a study to test whether a certain vitamin (vitamin X) increases energy levels in the elderly. First, the group would state their main hypothesis explicitly. It would probably be articulated in the following way – giving vitamin X to a group of elderly people will increase their energy level more than not giving them vitamin X. Having decided on the question to be answered, the team would go on to plan each operation of the study systematically. However, before carrying out the actual investigation, the team would also need to define the various aspects of the set hypothesis operationally. For instance, *elderly* and *energy level* would be specified in a way to permit quantification. Let us say that, after some consideration, they decided on 65 years and over as elderly and that energy level was to be measured as time spent on any non-sedentary activity carried out inside or outside the home. All activities could be monitored by means of a daily diary in which subjects indicated time spent on sedentary and non-sedentary activities under the assumption that the more non-sedentary activities engaged in, the higher the energy level (an assumption as hypothetical as the team!).

After more discussion, exact procedural details would be arrived at. Subjects over the age of 65 would be canvassed and randomly assigned to one of two treatment procedures: (1) one group (the experimental group) would be given vitamin X for a period of time expected to be long enough to produce results; and (2) under the same regimen, the other group (the control group) would be given a pill in every way comparable to vitamin X except that it would contain an inert substance. Medication containing an inert substance is called a placebo. It has been demonstrated repeatedly that only part of any drug's effect is due to its direct action on body chemistry (Claridge 1970; Shapiro & Morris 1978). The remainder is attributed to a host of other variables referring to attitudes and expectancies of clients and/or those of their advisers, as well as to the conditions under which treatment is administered. In the hypothetical study so far described, a placebo would ensure that both groups received equivalent treatment, making significant differences between their energy levels attributable to vitamin X and not extraneous factors. The best way to eliminate biases on the part of both experimenter and subject in drug trials is to administer treatment under the *double-blind* condition. The condition exists when both experimenter and subject are ignorant of who takes the active drug and who takes the placebo. To achieve a double-blind condition, it is necessary to solicit the help of someone not directly involved in the trials. The uninvolved person assigns treatments randomly according to a code which is not broken until the end of the evaluation. In therapy investigations, double-blind conditions are impossible to achieve because therapists cannot be blind to the treatment they minister their clients even though clients may not know that they are receiving a placebo therapy (*single-blind*).

Other problems are inherent in psychotherapy research, such as those relating to the identification and description of potentially effective therapy ingredients since it is clear that the complexities of both clients and their therapists need to be understood if treatment effects are not to be obscured completely. Criteria on which efficacy is to be judged have also been subjected to much debate without agreement being achieved.

The literature reporting the effects of psychotherapy has taken many forms, varying greatly as to scientific merit. A logical progression is often seen, starting with a case report in which a therapist described a certain procedure and its effect on one client, followed by group studies where the same procedure is applied on groups of homogeneous clients, providing results which allow generalizations to be made regarding therapeutic outcome. It is not always possible to conduct as ideal experiments in field studies as one would wish. In this context, studies conducted in clinical settings are considered to be field studies. Campbell (1957) introduced the term *quasi-experiments* to describe comparisons made in field settings with groups differing from each other in ways other than treatment conditions. The task of the researcher who attempts to interpret the results of quasi-experiments is that of separating the effects of a treatment procedure from subject variables which may have made experimental and control groups unequivalent. For instance, in the hypothetical example presented above, (let us say) that the body weight of the subjects was found to be more closely related to the performance of sedentary/non-sedentary activities than vitamin X. This finding would suggest a new investigation in which the body weight of the subjects would need to be controlled when assigning subjects to the different treatment groups. At this stage, it should be pointed out that the term *control* is used in different senses in research design. Cook and Campbell (1979) isolated three meanings for control. The first aspect of control refers to situational factors (therapy procedures); the second, to clear definitions of subjects' characteristics (diagnoses and any other relevant client characteristics, i.e., sex, age or demographic data) – *who* is receiving *what* treatment. Thirdly, any particular or contextual factors likely to affect the results in such a way as to obscure treatment effects must be considered; the non-specific/specific treatment factors alluded to earlier (e.g., expectancy) are instances of areas needing specific controls. Cook and Campbell (1979) stated the functions of control in the following way:

The three senses of control all involve ruling out threats to valid inference. In the first sense, the experimenter's control over the research environment serves as an omnibus means of ruling out threats, so much so that in some natural sciences the particular threats being ruled out need never be explicated and considered individually. It is as though they are handled automatically. In the second sense, control over the independent variable helps to separate effects of the treatment and of correlates of the treatment. With random assignment this unconfounding may once again be so automatic that the threats being ruled out need never be explicated individually. In the third sense, awareness of single threats is paramount, and research design becomes a matter of identifying the relevant threats and ruling them out through research design or through the constructs that are validly measured. Whatever its manifestation, the major function of control is the same: to rule out threats to valid inference. (A second function is to add precision, the ability to detect true effects of smaller magnitude.) However, since experimentation in field settings cannot readily use control in our first sense, but must use it in the last two senses, we can readily anticipate that causal inference will be much more problematic in field than in laboratory settings.

It might be thought that control in either of the first two senses can be discarded and that the research can instead explicate and measure all the relevant threats to valid inference. However, the importance of using experimental methods in less controlled field settings become clear after many attempts were made to infer causation from descriptive studies that were not experimental in form and that followed the logic of conceptualizing, measuring, and attempting to control statistically for threats (Cook & Campbell 1979, *Quasi-Experimentation*, Rand McNally: 8–9).

The first large-scale examination of the disparate literature reporting outcome of psychotherapy was carried out by Eysenck (1952). The results which emerged from his stringent examination were startling to many psychotherapists and uncomplimentary to psychotherapy, particularly to psychoanalysis. Rachman and Wilson (1980) attempted to summarize Eysenck's argument as it was presented in 1952 and extended in 1960 and 1969. Major methodological shortcomings were reported by Eysenck, particularly that few of the studies he found to review included adequate controls. Because of this, Eysenck was obliged to derive a baseline to compare benefit accrued from having received psychotherapy as opposed to not having received psychotherapy. He settled on a *best available estimate* of remissions which occurred in the absence of therapy based on earlier data provided by two other critics of psychotherapy (Denker 1946; Landis 1937). It was possible to conclude from their evidence that roughly two out of three individuals presenting with neurotic disorders would be recovered within two years even without receiving any form of treatment. These figures were supplemented in the 1960 study by others provided by Shepherd and Gruenberg (1957) who also concluded that the average duration of a neurosis was between one and two years.

The first evaluation carried out by Eysenck included 24 studies including over 7,000 cases of clients treated for a variety of neurotic disorders. He carried out an analysis based on global estimates categorized into four levels of improvement, ranging from cured or much improved to unimproved. He subsequently concluded that only 44 per cent of clients treated by psychoanalysis improved significantly compared with 64 per cent of clients who had received an eclectic type of psychotherapy. Both psychotherapy groups did less well than clients who had been treated custodially or by their GPs. The latter had shown a 72 per cent improvement rate. It appeared that receiving psychotherapy (a time-consuming and costly procedure) was less effective than either being treated minimally or not treated at all when one suffered from a neurotic problem. Eysenck admitted that he had had to use his own judgement when classifying clients according to diagnosis and degree of improvement and that many clients undergoing psychoanalysis had dropped out of treatment prematurely. However, when the attrition rate for psychoanalysis was taken under consideration, its recovery rate was increased to 66 per cent, a rate comparable to the effect obtained from eclectic psychotherapy, although not above the established baseline. In his two later studies, Eysenck (1960, 1969) carried out subsequent evaluations, including a wider range of clients than he had in 1952, along with controlled studies but his conclusions remained largely unchanged, leaving the onus for proof of psychotherapeutic effectiveness on those who advocate it. Rachman and Wilson (1980) summarized Eysenck's various findings into eight major conclusions:

1   When untreated neurotic control groups are compared with experimental groups of neurotic patients treated by means of psychotherapy, both groups recover to approximately the same extent.

2   When soldiers who have suffered a neurotic breakdown and have not received psychotherapy are compared with soldiers who have received psychotherapy, the chances of the two groups returning to duty are approximately equal.

3   When neurotic soldiers are separated from the service, their chances of recovery are not affected by their receiving or not receiving psychotherapy.

4   Civilian neurotics who are treated by psychotherapy recover or improve to approximately the same extent as similar neurotics receiving no psychotherapy.

5   Children suffering from emotional disorders and treated by psychotherapy recover or improve to approximately the same extent as similar children not receiving psychotherapy.

6   Neurotic patients treated by means of psychotherapeutic procedures based on learning theory improve significantly more quickly than do patients treated by means of psychoanalysis or eclectic psychotherapy, or not treated by psychotherapy at all.

7   Neurotic patients treated by psychoanalytic psychotherapy do not improve more quickly than patients treated by means of eclectic psychotherapy, and may improve less quickly when account is taken of the large proportion of patients breaking off treatment.

8   With the single exception of psychotherapeutic methods based on learning theory, results of published research with military and civilian neurotics, and with both adults and children, suggest that the therapeutic effects of psychotherapy are small or non-existent, and do not in any demonstrable way add to the non-specific effects

of routine medical treatment, or to such events as occur in patients' everyday life experience (Rachman & Wilson 1980, *The Effect of Psychotherapy*, Pergamon: 21).

In the light of the discouraging findings which emerged from Eysenck's evaluations, it was not surprising to find him and others such as Wolpe (1958) wishing to explore an alternative method of psychological intervention based on a more solid foundation. This alternative was found in behaviour therapy. Before going on to an evaluation of behaviour therapy in the context of psychotherapy research, some mention will be made of the various arguments raised to counteract Eysenck's criticisms.

In support of psychotherapy

Much was made of the fact that the studies Eysenck reviewed were flawed, a fact readily acknowledged by Eysenck himself. It was clear that cases which were compared were not matched for illness, there was seldom adequate definition of problems treated, interventions lacked clear specification, follow-up details were seldom available and outcome measures usually depended on the psychotherapist involved in treatment. Another criticism related to the use of group statistics to estimate average levels of improvement. In other words, if a number of individuals improve while others get worse, taking the average of the group on measures of outcome will obscure this fact. This concept of *average therapeutic effects* was proposed by Bergin (1966). Truax and Carkhuff (1967) extended the argument by attempting to find the variables determining positive or negative outcome in the characteristics of the therapists themselves. Unfortunately, neither of these promising leads were supported by later studies (Parloff, Waskow & Wolfe 1978; Rachman & Wilson 1980).

The spontaneous remission rate calculated by Eysenck in 1952 is unlikely to apply equally well to all so-called neurotic disorders. For instance, Rachman (1971b) suggested a league table in which neurotic depression would be more likely to remit than, for instance, obsessional-compulsive disorders and hypochondriasis. Clinicians are confronted repeatedly by clients who come forward for help, having suffered with a neurotic type problem well over two years. However, we are still not in a strong position to improve on the estimates of remission made in the 1940s and 1950s (Rachman & Wilson 1980).

A strong argument was made against outcome research, which is designed to compare one psychological therapy as practised by adherents of a particular therapeutic school with another representing a different school, for instance, psychoanalysis and behaviour therapy, eclectic psychotherapy and psychoanalysis or simply psychotherapy and behaviour therapy. Kiesler (1966) pointed to a number of faulty assumptions inherent in this type of comparison. He labelled these fallacies *uniformity assumption myths*. One way to fall prey to these myths is to assume that all therapists representing any one of the many therapy schools give uniform treatment. Rachman and Wilson (1980) added that there is no routine treatment as such and that: 'Proper evaluation of comparative outcome research necessitates detailed information on the specific method used, their credibility for the subjects, and the time and treatment personnel involved in therapy' (Rachman & Wilson 1980: 107). Outcome therapy research is based on comparisons between two measurement points, before (pre) and after (post) therapy. However, it is also necessary to look at what is going on during therapy to identify its effective processes, that is, those which contribute significantly to positive outcome. Orlinsky and Howard (1978), in their exposition of the relation of process to outcome in psychotherapy, illustrated their arguments by taking social relationship as a typical process of psychotherapy, one directly derived from a definition of psychotherapy which included that it was *a relation among persons*. After an extensive review, they found psychotherapy research to be plagued by five basic problems: problem of descriptive specificity, fair sample, causal inference, outcome evaluation and prescriptive utility. The next section will be aimed at showing how researchers evaluating behaviour therapy have attempted to overcome these problems.

Behaviour therapy research

Reference to the phenomenal growth in the research and practice of behaviour therapy was made in the first chapter of this book. There is little doubt that the behavioural approach has succeeded in remaining first and foremost a scientifically based approach to psychological treatment. The task of providing a detailed analysis of the outcome evidence under one cover is now deemed impossible. However, more comprehensive reviews than are possible in a book of this kind exist elsewhere (Bellack, Hersen & Kazdin 1982; Hersen & Bellack 1985; Kazdin & Wilson 1978; Rachman & Wilson 1980). During an invited address presented at the 14th Annual Convention of the Association for Advancement of Behavior Therapy, Marks (1981) declared: 'This decade marks the coming of age of the discipline of behavioral treatment. It has finally been recognized that behavioral psychotherapy is indeed empirical and clinical and that it can stand on its own without having to borrow respectability by claimimg antecedents from other areas' (Marks 1981, Toward an empirical clinical science, *Behavior Therapy*: 63). He went on to qualify his statement thus: 'In behavioural psychotherapy the clinical environment constitutes the research environment. Systematic treatment with measurement enables us both to help the patient and to advance science at the same time. Every patient is a unique experiment, the potential start of a new treatment approach, and a new theoretical issue' (Marks 1981: 68). With reference to the list of problems encountered in psychotherapy research provided by Orlinsky and Howard (1978), examples will follow to show how the *empirical clinician* has tackled the demands for descriptive specificity, fair sample, causal inference, outcome evaluation and prescriptive utility.

Descriptive specificity

Kazdin and Wilson (1978) reflected a concensus of opinion among behaviour therapists, when they judged outcome studies to be of little value in the absence of sound process studies designed to answer fundamental questions about the workings of a specific treatment. They discussed different research strategies used to evaluate the efficacy of therapy, stressing that the appropriateness of each strategy is determined by the hypothesis being tested. These included: 'the treatment package, constructive, dismantling, parametric, comparative, client-therapist variation, and internal structure or process strategies' (Kazdin & Wilson 1978, *Evaluation of Behavior Therapy*, Ballinger: 138).

The treatment package concept stems from the idea that a treatment is described in such precise terms that its various components are clearly distinguished from each other. Systematic desensitization described in Chapter 3 is a good example of a treatment package. The treatment package approach is often the first evaluative step to test whether the package *in toto* is able to change the condition for which it is given, compared with when it is not given or with a placebo treatment. In contrast, the constructive treatment strategy involves adding selected components to an existing treatment procedure to test whether the addition enhances efficacy. The dismantling strategy is used to evaluate the effectiveness of each ingredient separately. The constructive or dismantling strategies can be applied to support or disconfirm particular theories regarding change. In the parametric treatment strategy, specific components of the treatment procedure are varied, for instance, varying number and spacing of sessions or length of exposure time, to discover the best formula to achieve lasting change. The problems inherent in the comparative treatment strategy research were covered earlier. Comparative studies can be used to compare two or more treatments that are conceptually different as well as variations of the same technique. Recently, the type of comparative study which tests for the most efficacious treatment from known alternatives or pits a new treatment against an established one, has been strongly advocated (Basham 1986; Kazdin 1986; Parloff 1986). Before going on to client-therapist variation strategies, it should be mentioned that the need for accurate specification of treatment procedures is being increasingly met by *manualization*. Ideally, this means that a *manual* is written specifying all aspects of a particular programme in detail. Therapists are then trained to implement the techniques so described before their adherence to the manual is assessed under treatment conditions (Stiles, Shapiro & Elliott 1986).

Client or therapist variation strategy was initially used in studies of therapies other than behavioural. However, it is increasingly recognized by behaviour therapists that both clients and their therapists have characteristics which interact with treatment procedures to affect outcome. It is necessary to identify these important dimensions first. For instance, certain types of therapist behaviour, such as the degree of influence exerted on clients, can be varied by the same therapist across a group of clients to evaluate whether influence tactics contribute to improvement. With regard to client characteristics, it was demonstrated in Chapter 5 that clients who showed their anxiety somatically responded better to somatic than non-somatic procedures. Outcome and process studies were dichotomized earlier in this chapter, but they are not always so clearly differentiated. Many studies in the literature view changes during treatment sessions as interim measures of outcome. Greenberg (1986) viewed the process of change during therapy as reflected by three types of outcome or change measures, i.e., immediate outcome, intermediate outcome and ultimate or final outcome. He went on to say that all these measures need to be related to each other to provide a complete picture of the change process occurring as a result of therapy.

Fair sample

It is universally agreed that the results of therapy research should be generalizable to typical client populations. Unfortunately this is often put in question because of a tendency for research to be conducted in unrepresentative university settings with easily available subjects having a limited range of problems. The use of analogue studies, so-called because they are carried out under conditions that only resemble or approximate the clinical situation, has probably been greater with regard to behaviour therapy than any other therapy. When combing the behaviour therapy literature, it is not uncommon to find studies of students who were treated for mild phobic problems. Although widely criticized, these analogue studies have continued because they meet control conditions more readily than field studies. Kazdin (1978b) defended the use of analogue studies in the following way:

> An investigation invariably will be an analogue by the very nature of experimental research. The alternative questions of interest seem to be the extent in which treatment research deviates from the clinical situation, along what dimensions, and whether the manner in which there are differences, makes research a relatively strong or weak test of treatment in relation to the likely results in a clinical situation ... Increasing similarity of an investigation to the clinical situation for a given dimension does not necessarily argue for greater generality of the results from the research to the clinical setting. Whether standing of a study on a given dimension is relevant to generality of the results needs to be determined empirically (Kazdin 1978b, Evaluating the generality of findings in analogue therapy research, *Journal of Consulting and Clinical Psychology*: 684–5).

Criticism has also been made of the increasing use of media advertisements to obtain subjects for psychotherapy research. Krupnick, Shea and Elkin (1986) compared studies of solicited clients with studies of non-solicited clients. They found similar responses to treatment in both groups but also consistent differences between the groups on pre-treatment measures regarding precipitants and duration of symptoms. Solicited clients were more likely not to have experienced precipitants and to have suffered their problems for longer periods than non-solicited clients. The meaning of these differences remains unclear and, in view of the small number of studies available for inspection, the authors cautioned against premature interpretation of their results.

Causal inference

The primary aim of psychotherapy research is to determine causal relations between process and outcome variables. In other words, to what extent and in what way do the components which make up the therapy experience contribute to the desired changes. The empirical clinician seeks to find ways of ruling out plausible alternative explanations of therapeutic outcome. This is not so easy when clients are submitted to a variety of influences outside treatment. In the absence of all the necessary controls which would make causal inferences almost certain, psychotherapy researchers must probe probalistic causal connections. In this way, they are able to say that changes in a client's behaviour are *probably* consequences of a certain behaviour therapy programme.

Outcome evaluation

Behaviour therapists have made outcome target specificity central to evaluation, whether the evaluation involves a single case or a group of clients. In the past, therapy outcome research was based primarily on group studies where average amount of change was liable to obscure individual differences between clients. For this and other reasons regarding the nature of clinical practice, the group approach to evaluating therapy has been found less than satisfactory by a number of researchers, who have developed strategies to enable rigorous evaluations of single cases (Hersen & Barlow 1976; Hersen 1982). Whether one is evaluating a group of clients or using single-case experimental methodology, it is widely agreed that the taking of multi-faceted outcome measures is advisable. Behaviourists believe that these measures should reflect different perspectives (e.g., client's, therapist's, significant others), different facets of the individual (e.g., affect, cognitions, behaviour), and different methods of assessments (e.g., self-report, clinician ratings, direct observation) (Kazdin 1986). However, it should be stressed that the major criterion for evaluating change in clinical research is whether therapy has helped the client change problematic behaviour to a degree which enhances his/her everyday functioning. Therefore, statistical significance should not be considered outside clinical significance. In addition, it follows that durability of change must be evaluated by means of a follow-up assessment carried out some period of time after termination of treatment.

It has not been easy to make sense of the increasing output of studies evaluating the efficacy of psychological interventions. Recent reviewers of psychotherapy studies have attempted to bring some order to the field by adopting one of two strategies, the box-score approach or meta-analysis. The box-score strategy is based on dichotomizing outcome measurements as being statistically significant or not, whatever their provenance. Based on this simple classification, outcome is qualified as being *better than, worse than,* or *not different from* an alternative therapy to which it is compared. Meta-analysis was proposed by Smith and Glass (1977) as an alternative to the box-score method. It is based on an *effect size* as the basic unit of analysis calculated from the mean difference between the treated and control group clients divided by the standard deviation of the control group. Although both methods have helped to summarize large quantities of disparate data, they have also been subjected to criticism (Fiske 1983; Kazdin & Wilson 1978; Shapiro & Shapiro 1982; Strube & Hartman 1982).

Prescriptive utility

This is closely tied to the concept of fair sample. Although behaviour therapists have found more experimental studies into the efficacy of their methods than therapists of other schools, it has nevertheless been noted that psychotherapy research has failed to influence the majority of practitioners (including behaviour therapists sampled) in the field (Cohen,

Sargent & Sechrest 1986; Morrow-Bradley & Elliott 1986). With this in mind, a recent handbook of behaviour therapy was addressed more specifically to clinicians than previous handbooks (Hersen & Bellack 1985). It included relevant research and clinical information regarding behavioural programmes for anxiety disorders, depression, schizophrenia and a variety of other life problems, testifying to the wide utility of the behavioural approach.

Evaluation of Mrs A's treatment programme

Salient aspects of the programme were discussed in previous chapters with reference to Mrs A's progress through the five intensive therapist-assisted sessions. Suffice to reaffirm that all decisions regarding the design of the programme were dictated by the experimental literature with an eye to cost/benefit issues regarding both client and therapist time. In summary, the experimental literature favoured exposure *in vivo*, long exposure sessions as opposed to short ones and coping techniques to match for anxiety responding. The literature also related self-efficacy to performance, self-control to self-efficacy and stress inoculation to longer-lasting results. Ethical considerations as well as theoretical ones determined the educational basis for the programme. Multi-faceted measures were taken before, during, at the end of the five-week therapist-assisted programme, after five more weeks (ten weeks from the beginning) and after six months. The measures were found to be a useful way of giving feedback to clients during treatment (see Ch. 6) as well as for evaluating the programme. The measures taken were primarily based on the clients' rating of their behaviour as well as of their feelings. Since the programme is part of an ongoing evaluation, each group is analysed separately as well as added to the pool of information which is accumulating as each treatment programme takes place. Outcome was measured as the differences between pre-treatment and post-treatment evaluation and changes were monitored between sessions to identify active processes occurring during therapy. To illustrate the evaluation process which was conducted in parallel with Mrs A's treatment, a brief account of some of our pre/post measures along with an indication of some of the types of question we are trying to answer will be given.

All clients were asked to complete the Marks and Mathews

Table 7.1 Mrs A's Self-efficacy ratings

10 quite uncertain	20	30	40	50 moderately certain	60	70	80	90	100 certain		
										Can do	Confidence
1. Walk two blocks from home alone.										Yes	70
2.											
3. Going to church alone, stand at back 1/2 hour.										Yes	50
4.											
5. Go into uncrowded store with small shopping list.										Yes	60
6.											
7. Go in bank line-up, stay 10 minutes.										Yes	50
8.											
9. Go into crowded shop, quick check-out.										Yes	50
10.											
11. Go on bus for 15 minute journey.										Yes	40
12.											
13. Go into crowded shop with long shopping list.										No	30
14.											
15. Go visit a friend who lives 3/4 miles outside city in friend's car.										No	40
16.											

Fear Questionnaire (Marks & Mathews 1979) because the questionnaire includes an avoidance scale which has a separate agoraphobic avoidance scale, a mood scale (anxiety/depression) and a disability scale. In our view, these scales are suitable to give a good indication of clinical

Table 7.1 continued

10 quite uncertain	20	30	40	50 moderately certain	60	70	80	90	100 certain		

		Can do	Confidence
17.	Go to cinema.	No	40
18.			
19.	Go walk alone 1/2 hour.	No	30
20.			
21.	Take bus to friend's home.	No	20
22.			
23.	Wait in long line-up at bank until served.	No	20
24.			
25.	Go to church sit in middle.	No	30
26.			
27.	Go to church sit in front.	No	10
28.			
29.	Go to communion.	No	10
30.			

'Can do' = 40%

Efficacy expectations = 36.67%

improvement. The mood scale was supplemented by the Beck depression inventory (Beck *et al.* 1961). The use of the microanalysis procedure devised by Bandura (1977) to evaluate each item of clients' hierarchy was discussed earlier. To illustrate the use of the technique, Mrs A's self-efficacy ratings given during the first session of the programme are found in Table 7.1. An evaluation of some aspects of the particular programme which included Mrs A is published elsewhere (Liddell *et al.* 1986). In the report in questions, 'pre' and 'post' results were given for clients who completed the programme with Mrs A. On the self-efficacy measures, the pre-treatment evaluation mean on 'can do' was 45.88 per cent (SD = 15.39) while the efficacy expectation mean was 43.38 per cent (SD = 9.12). After ten weeks, the averages had risen to 87.25 per cent (SD = 22.26) and 70.63 per cent (SD = 12.55) respectively. The other outcome measures also showed both statistical and clinical significance since the clients changed their disability perception on the fear questionnaire from an average of 6.37 (based on 0–8 ratings which ranged from no phobia present (0) to very severely disturbing/disabling (8). The 6+ rating indicated that the phobic symptoms of the clients before treatment were, on average, markedly disturbing/disabling. On the other hand, the post-treatment average of 3+ located them somewhere between slightly disturbing and definitely disturbing/disabling. It is evident from the standard deviations that there was great variability within the clients making up this group. One of our projects is to look for the best predictors of outcome from our between-session measures. Another ongoing study is an examination of the false beliefs concerning agoraphobia our clients bring to the clinic. This was stimulated by a recent paper on differentiation between classically conditioned and cognitively based neurotic fears which Wolpe brought to our attention (Wolpe, Lande, McNally & Schotte 1985). As a measure of false beliefs, we are examining the answers given by clients to the test we based on Mathews's *et al., Client's Manual* (Ch. 6).

There is no doubt that our past clients have taught us a

great deal which we are attempting to put into practice to help future clients. In other words and to paraphrase Marks (1981), our clinic has been our laboratory in which clients are appreciated and treated as individuals.

Chapter 8

Conclusion

It is hoped that the discussions carried out in previous chapters have helped to provide the reader with insights into the practice of behaviour therapy. It is also hoped that the aim of showing the behavioural approach as a broad spectrum one has been achieved. Its breadth of techniques and the breadth of problems successfully remedied by behaviour therapy should never obscure the fact that clients are given careful individual analyses before undergoing treatment. It is true that decisions regarding the choice of behavioural interventions are empirically based but they are also made according to the wishes and needs of clients. Programmes are increasingly more often planned to give clients generalizable skills rather than tight control over small aspects of behaviour. Behaviour was understood in the broadest sense to include cognition and physiology as well as overt motoric behaviour. Various models to explain behaviour change have stimulated methodological advances in the evaluation of psychological treatment. Initially, behaviour therapy was seen to do remarkably well in comparative studies when compared with other approaches but, in studies where good controls were in operation, it did not keep its margin (Sloane, Staples, Cristol, Yorkston & Whipple 1975; Stiles, Shapiro & Elliott 1986). It is likely that other psychological therapies share common ingredients which need to be recognized and put to the test in fine-grained process research studies.

What's in a name?

Behaviour therapy has had problems with its name in the past. Behaviour therapy and behaviour modification are now used synonymously. How does behaviour therapy/ modification relate to psychotherapy? The term behavioural psychotherapy adopted in the UK makes it clearly a form of psychotherapy. However, psychotherapy has had very narrow connotations in some circles. For instance, it has been used to refer to therapy of the type practised by psychoanalysts or other therapists who share a similar psychodynamic approach. Since it is now evident that many types of psychotherapy have a positive effect, the new label of *psychosocial intervention* appears to parallel a detente among traditional enemies. In any case, the broad philosophy which unites behaviour therapists will make it easy for them to adopt the new label if need be.

Further readings

The references were chosen with a bias towards the prospective clinician. The first two references chosen are the two special issues of psychology periodicals devoted to psychotherapy research: *American Psychologist,* **41**, 1986 and *Journal of Consulting and Clinical Psychology,* **54**, 1986. These two journals should place behaviour therapy firmly in the context of psychosocial interventions. The next two books illustrate the complexity and importance of behavioural assessment: Cormier, W. H. and Cormier, L. S. (1985) *Interviewing Strategies for Helpers* 2nd edn. Monterey, CA: Brooks/Cole; and Hersen, M. and Bellack, A. S. (1981) *Behavioral Assessment: A Practical Handbook*, 2nd edn. New York: Pergamon. Two other handbooks were chosen because of their comprehensiveness: Bellack, A. S., Hersen, M. and Kazdin, A. E. (eds) (1982) *International Handbook of Behavior Modification and Therapy*. New York: Plenum; and Hersen, M. and Bellack, A. S. (eds) (1985) *Handbook of Clinical Behavior Therapy with Adults*. New York: Plenum.

Finally, two books which address fundamental issues round off the selection: Reiss, S. and Bootzin, R. R. (1985) *Theoretical Issues in Behavior Therapy*. Orlando: Academic Press; and Wilson, G. T. and Franks, C. M. (1982) *Contemporary Behavior Therapy: Conceptual and Empirical Foundations*. New York: Guilford.

References

Ad Hoc Committee on Classification of Headache (1962) Classification of headache, *Journal of American Medical Association,* **179**, 127–8.

Akhtar, S., Wig, N. N., Varma, V. K., Pershad, D. and Verma, S. K. (1975) A phenomenological analysis of symptoms in obsessive-compulsive neurosis, *British Journal of Psychiatry,* **127**, 342–8.

Alexander, F. (1950) *Psychosomatic Medicine.* New York: Norton.

American Psychiatric Association (1980) *Diagnostic and Statistical Manual of Mental Disorders,* 3rd edn. Washington, DC: American Psychiatric Association.

Association for Advancement of Behavior Therapy (1977) Ethical issues for human services, *Behavior Therapy,* **8**, 5–7.

Ayllon, T. and Azrin, N. H. (1968) *The Token Economy: A Motivational System for Therapy and Rehabilitation.* New York: Appleton-Century-Crofts.

Ayllon, T. and Kelly, K. (1972) Effects of reinforcement on standardized test performance, *Journal of Applied Behavior Analysis,* **4**, 477–84.

Bacon, M. and Poppen, R. (1985) A behavioral analysis of diaphramatic breathing and its effects on peripheral temperature, *Journal of Behavior Therapy and Experimental Psychiatry,* **16**, 15–21.

Bandura, A. (1969) *Principles of Behavior Modification.* New York: Holt, Rinehart and Winston.

Bandura, A. (1971) Psychotherapy based on modeling principles, in A. E. Bergin and S. L. Garfield (eds), *Handbook of Psychotherapy and Behavior Change.* New York: Wiley.

Bandura, A. (1977) Self-efficacy: Toward a unifying theory of behavioral change, *Psychological Review,* **84,** 191–215.

Barlow, D. (ed.) (1981) *Behavioral Assessment of Adult Disorders.* New York, Guilford.

Barlow, D. H. and **Wolfe, B. E.** (1981) Behavioral approaches to anxiety disorders: A report on the NIMH-SUNY, Albany, research conference, *Journal of Consulting and Clinical Psychology,* **49,** 448–54.

Basham, R. B. (1986) Scientific and practical advantages of comparative design in psychotherapy outcome research, *Journal of Consulting and Clinical Psychology,* **54,** 88–94.

Beck, A. T., Rush, A. R. Shaw, B. F. and **Emery, G.** (1979) *Cognitive Therapy of Depression.* New York: Wiley.

Beck, A. T., Ward, C. H., Mendelsohn, M., Mock, J. and **Erbaugh, J.** (1961) An inventory for measuring depression, *Archives of General Psychiatry,* **4,** 561–71.

Beech, H. R. (1969) *Changing Man's Behavior.* Harmondsworth: Penguin.

Beech, H. R. and **Liddell, A.** (1974) Decision-making, mood states and ritualistic behavior among obsessional patients, in H. R. Beech (ed.), *Obsessional States.* London: Methuen.

Beech, H. R. and **Vaughn, M.** (1978) *Behavioural Treatment of Obsessional States.* Chichester: Wiley.

Behavioural Psychotherapy: Editorial (1983) What's in a name, *Behavioural Psychotherapy,* **11,** 201–3.

Bellack, A. S., Hersen, M. and **Kazdin, A. E.** (eds) (1982) *International Handbook of Behavior Modification and Therapy.* New York: Plenum.

Bergin, A. E. (1966) Some implications of psychotherapeutic research for therapeutic practice, *Journal of Abnormal Psychology,* **71,** 235–46.

Bergin, A. E. and **Garfield, S. L.** (eds) (1971) *Handbook of Psychotherapy and Behavior Change.* New York: Wiley.

Bernstein, L. and **Bernstein, R. S.** (1980) *Interviewing: A Guide for Health Professionals,* 3rd edn. New York: Appleton-Century-Crofts.

Bernstein, D. and **Borkovec, T. D.** (1973) *Progressive Relaxation Training: A Manual for the Helping Professions.* Champaign, IL: Research Press.

Blanchard, E. B. and **Andrasik, F.** (1982) Psychological assessment and treatment of headache: Recent developments and emerging issues, *Journal of Consulting and Clinical Psychology,* **50,** 859–79.

Blanchard, E. B., Andrasik, F., Evans, D. D., Neff, D. F., Appelbaum, K. A. and Rodichok, L. D. (1985) Behavioral treatment of 250 chronic headache patients: A clinical replication series, *Behavior Therapy,* **16,** 308–27.

Borkovec, T. D., Robinson, E., Pruzinsky, T. and DePree, J. A. (1983) Preliminary exploration of worry: Some characteristics and processes, *Behaviour Research and Therapy,* **21,** 9–16.

Borkovec, T. D. and Sides, J. K. (1979) Critical procedural variables related to the physiological effects of progressive relaxation, *Behaviour Research and Therapy,* **17,** 119–25.

Breuer, J. and Freud, S. (1893). On the psychical mechanisms of hysterical phenomena: Preliminary communication, in M. Hamilton (ed.) (1967) *Abnormal Psychology.* Harmondsworth: Penguin.

Budzynski, T., Stoyva, J. and Adler, C. (1970) Feedback-induced muscle relaxation: Application to tension headache, *Journal of Behavior Therapy and Experimental Psychiatry,* **1,** 205–11.

Campbell, D. T. (1957) Factors relevant to the validity of experiments in social settings, *Psychological Bulletin,* **54,** 297–312.

Cannon, W. E. (1942) 'Voodoo' death, *American Anthropologist,* **44,** 169–82.

Cautela, J. R. (1979) Covert conditioning: Assumptions and Procedures, in D. Upper and J. R. Cautela (eds), *Covert Conditioning.* New York: Pergamon.

Chambless, D. L. and Goldstein, A. J. (1982) *Agoraphobia: Multiple Perspectives on Theory and Treatment.* New York: Wiley.

Churchland, P. M. (1984) *Matter and Consciousness.* Cambridge, MA: The Massachusetts Institute of Technology Press.

Ciminero, A. R. (1977) Behavioral assessment: An overview, in A. R. Ciminero, K. S. Calhoun and H. E. Adams (eds), *Handbook of Behavioral Assessment.* New York: Wiley.

Ciminero, A. R., Calhoun, K. S. and Adams, H. E. (eds) (1977) *Handbook of Behavioral Assessment.* New York: Wiley.

Claridge, G. (1970) *Drugs and Human Behaviour.* Harmondsworth: Penguin.

Claridge, G. (1973) Psychosomatic relations in physical disease, in H. J. Eysenck (ed.) *Handbook of Abnormal Psychology.* London: Pitman Medical.

Clark, D. M. and Hemsley, D. R. (1982) Effects of hyperventilation: Individual variability and its relation to personality, *Journal of Behavior Therapy and Experimental Psychiatry,* **13,** 41–7.

Clark, D. M., Salkovskis, P. M. and Chalkley, A. J. (1985) Respiratory control as a treatment for panic attacks, *Journal of Behavior Therapy and Experimental Psychiatry,* **16,** 23–30.

Clay, C. J. (1983) A portable data collection system, *The Behavior Therapist,* **6,** 128.

Cleary, P. J. (1980) A checklist for life event research, *Journal of Psychosomatic Research,* **24,** 199–207.

Cohen, L. H., Sargent, M. M. and Sechrest, L. B. (1986) Use of psychotherapy research by professional psychologists, *American Psychologist,* **41,** 198–206.

Cone, J. D. (1981) Psychometric considerations, in M. Hersen and A. S. Bellack (eds), *Behavioral Assessment: A Practical Handbook,* 2nd edn. New York: Pergamon.

Cone, J. D. and Hawkins, R. P. (eds) (1977) *Behavioral Assessment: New Directions in Clinical Psychology.* New York: Brunner/Mazel.

Cook, T. D. and Campbell, D. T. (1979) *Quasi-Experimentation: Design & Analysis Issues for Field Settings.* Chicago: Rand McNally.

Cormier, W. H. and Cormier, L. S. (1985) *Interviewing Strategies for Helpers,* 2nd edn. Monterey, CA: Brooks/Cole.

Denker, P. (1946) The results of treatment of psychoneuroses by the G.P., *New York State Journal of Medicine,* **46,** 2164–6.

DeRisi, W. J. and Butz, G. (1975) *Writing Behavioral Contracts.* Champaign, IL: Research Press.

Dohrenwend, B. S. and Dohrenwend, B. P. (1974) *Stressful Life Events.* New York: Wiley.

Doleys, D. M. and Bruno, J. (1982) Treatment of childhood medical disorders, in A. S. Bellack, M. Hersen and A. E. Kazdin (eds), *International Handbook of Behavior Modification and Therapy.* New York: Plenum.

Dollard, J. and Miller, N. E. (1950) *Personality and Psychotherapy.* New York: McGraw-Hill.

Ellis, A. (1962) *Reason and Emotion in Psychotherapy.* New York: Lyle Stuart.

Emmelkamp, P. M. G. (1982) Anxiety and fear, in A. S. Bellack, M. Hersen and A. E. Kazdin (eds), *International Handbook of Behavior Modification and Therapy.* New York: Plenum.

Eysenck, H. J. (1952) The effects of psychotherapy: An evaluation, *Journal of Consulting Psychology,* **16,** 319–24.

Eysenck, H. J. (1959) Learning theory and behaviour therapy, *Journal of Mental Science,* **104,** 61–75.

Eysenck, H. J. (1960) *Behaviour Therapy and the Neuroses*. Oxford: Pergamon.

Eysenck, H. J. (1969) *The Effects of Psychotherapy*. New York: Science House.

Eysenck, H. J. (1982) Neobehaviorist (S-R) theory, in G. T. Wilson and C. M. Franks (eds), *Contemporary Behavior Therapy: Conceptual and Empirical Foundations*. New York: Guilford.

Eysenck, H. J. and Eysenck, S. B. G. (1976) *Psychotism as a Dimension of Personality*. London: Hodder and Stoughton.

Eysenck, H. J. and Rachman, S. J. (1965) *The Causes and Cures of Neurosis*. London: Routledge & Kegan Paul.

Farrell, A. D. (1986) The microcomputer as a tool for behavioral assessment, *The Behavior Therapist*, **9**, 16–17.

Fiske, D. W. (1983) The meta-analytic revolution in outcome research, *Journal of Consulting and Clinical Psychology*, **51**, 65–70.

Fowles, D. C. (1984) Biological variables in psychopathology: A Psychobiological perspective, in H. E. Adams and P. B. Sutker (eds), *Comprehensive Handbook of Psychopathology*. New York: Plenum.

Freedman, A. M., Dornbush, R. L. and Shapiro, B. (1981) Anxiety: Here today and here tomorrow, *Comprehensive Psychiatry*, **22**, 44–53.

Friedman, J. M., Weiler, S. J., LoPiccolo, J. and Hogan, D. R. (1982). Sexual dysfunctions and their treatment: Current status, in A. S. Bellack, M. Hersen and A. E. Kazdin (eds), *International Handbook of Behavior Modification and Therapy*. New York: Plenum.

Garfield, S. L. (1978) Research on client variables in psychotherapy, in S. L. Garfield and A. E. Bergin (eds), *Handbook of Psychotherapy and Behavior Change*, 2nd edn. New York: Wiley.

Glaister, B. (1982) Muscle relaxation training for fear reduction of patients with psychological problems: A review of controlled studies, *Behaviour Research and Therapy*, **20**, 493–504.

Goldfried, M. R. (1982) Behavioral assessment: An overview, in A. S. Bellack, M. Hersen and A. E. Kazdin (eds), *Handbook of Behavior Modification and Therapy*. New York: Plenum.

Goldfried, M. R. and Linehan, M. M. (1977) Basic issues to behavioral assessment, in A. R. Ciminero, K. S. Calhoun and H. E. Adams (eds), *Handbook of Behavioral Assessment*. New York: Wiley.

Goldfried, M. R. and **Sprafkin, J. N.** (1976) Behavioral personality assessment, in R. C. Carson and J. W. Thibaut (eds), *Behavioral Approaches to Therapy*. Morristown, NJ: General Learning Press.

Goldiamond, E. (1965) Self-control procedures in personal behavior problems, *Psychological Reports,* **17,** 851–68.

Goldstein, A. J. and **Chambless, D. L.** (1978) A reanalysis of agoraphobia, *Behavior Therapy,* **9,** 47–59.

Goodwin, D. L. (1969) Consulting with the classroom teacher, in J. D. Krumboltz and C. E. Thoresen (eds), *Behavioral Counseling: Cases and Techniques.* New York: Holt, Rinehart and Winston.

Gray, J. A. (1985) A whole and its parts: Behaviour, the brain, cognition and emotion, *Bulletin of The British Psychological Society,* **38,** 99–112.

Greenberg, L. S. (1986) Change process research, *Journal of Consulting and Clinical Psychology,* **54,** 4–9.

Gurman, A. S. (1973) Treatment of a case of public-speaking anxiety by *in vivo* desensitization and cue-controlled relaxation, *Journal of Behavior Therapy and Experimental Psychiatry,* **4,** 51–4.

Gurnani, P. D. and **Vaughn, M.** (1981) Changes in frequency and distress during prolonged repetition of obsessional thoughts, *British Journal of Clinical Psychology,* **20,** 79–81.

Hamilton, M. (1967) Development of a rating scale for primary depressive illness, *British Journal of Social and Clinical Psychology,* **6,** 278–96.

Hart, D. S. (1986) Overview of special section on childhood obesity: Can psychologists help the obese child? *Canadian Psychology,* **27,** 260–1.

Haynes, S. N. (1978) *Principles of Behavioral Assessment.* New York: Gardner.

Heiman, J., LoPiccolo, L. and **LoPiccolo, J.** (1976) *Becoming Orgasmic: A Sexual Growth Program for Women.* Englewood Cliffs, NJ: Prentice-Hall.

Hersen, M. (1982) Single-case experimental design, in A. S. Bellack, M. Hersen and A. E. Kazdin (eds), *International Handbook of Behavior Modification and Therapy.* New York: Plenum.

Hersen, M. and **Barlow, D. H.** (1976) *Single Case Experimental Designs: Strategies for Studying Behavior Change.* New York: Pergamon.

Hersen, M. and **Bellack, A. S.** (eds) (1976) *Behavioral Assessment: A Practical Handbook.* New York: Pergamon.

Hersen, M. and **Bellack, A. S.** (eds) (1981) *Behavioral Assessment: A Practical Handbook,* 2nd edn. New York: Pergamon.

Hersen, M. and Bellack, A. S. (eds) (1985) *Handbook of Clinical Behavior Therapy with Adults.* New York: Plenum.

Hobbs, N. (1964) Mental health's third revolution, *American Journal of Orthopsychiatry,* **34,** 822–33.

Hodgson, R. and Rachman, S. (1974) II. Desynchrony in measures of fear, *Behaviour Research and Therapy,* **12,** 319–26.

Holmes, T. H. and Rahe, R. H. (1967) The social readjustment scale, *Journal of Psychosomatic Research,* **11,** 213–18.

Jobe, J. B., Sampson, J. B., Roberts, D. E. and Kelly, J. A. (1986) Comparison of behavioral treatments for Raynaud's disease, *Journal of Behavioral Medicine,* **9,** 89–96.

Jones, M. C. (1924) A laboratory study of fear: The case of Peter, *Pedagogical Seminary,* **31,** 308–15.

Kanfer, F. H. (1980) Self-managment methods, in F. H. Kanfer and A. P. Goldstein (eds), *Helping People to Change,* 2nd edn. New York: Pergamon.

Kanfer, F. H. and Philips, J. S. (1970) *Learning Foundations of Behavior Therapy.* New York: Wiley.

Kanfer, F. H. and Saslow, G. (1965) Behavioral analysis, *Archives of General Psychiatry,* **12,** 529–38.

Kanfer, F. H. and Saslow, G. (1969) Behavior diagnosis, in C. M. Franks (ed.), *Behavior Therapy: Appraisal and Status.* New York: McGraw-Hill.

Kanner, A. D., Coyne, J. C., Schaefer, C. and Lazarus, R. S. (1981) Comparison of two modes of stress measurement: Daily hassles and uplifts vs major life events, *Journal of Behavioral Medicine,* **4,** 1–39.

Kazdin, A. E. (1978a) *History of Behavior Modification.* Baltimore: University Park Press.

Kazdin, A. E. (1978b) Evaluating the generality of findings in analogue therapy research, *Journal of Consulting and Clinical Psychology,* **54,** 673–86.

Kazdin, A. E. (1979) Fictions, factions, and functions of behavior therapy, *Behavior Therapy,* **10,** 629–54.

Kazdin, A. E. (1982a) History of behavior modification, in A. S. Bellack, M. Hersen and A. E. Kazdin (eds), *International Handbook of Behavior Modification and Therapy.* New York: Plenum.

Kazdin, A. E. (1982b) Symptom substitution, generalization, and response covariation: Implications for psychotherapy outcome, *Psychological Bulletin,* **91,** 349–65.

Kazdin, A. E. (1986) Comparative outcome studies of psycho-therapy: Methodological issues and strategies, *Journal of Consulting and Clinical Psychology,* **54,** 95–105.

Kazdin, A. E. and Wilson, G. T. (1978) *Evaluation of Behavior Therapy: Issues, Evidence, and Research Strategies.* Cambridge, MA: Ballinger.

Kendall, P. C. (1984) Behavioral assessment and methodology, in G. T. Wilson, C. M. Franks, K. D. Brownell and P. C. Kendall (eds), *Annual Review of Behavior Therapy, 9.* New York: Guilford.

Kendall, P. C. and Hollon, S. (eds) (1979) *Cognitive-Behavioral Interventions: Theory, Research and Procedures.* New York: Academic Press.

Kendall, P. C., Plous, S. and Kratochwill, T. R. (1981) Science and behaviour therapy: A survey of research in the 1970s, *Behaviour Research and Therapy,* **19,** 517–24.

Kiesler, D. J. (1966) Some myths of psychotherapy research and the search for a paradigm, *Psychological Bulletin,* **65, 110**–36.

Krasner, L. (1971) Behavior therapy, *Annual Review of Psychology,* **22,** 483–532.

Krasner, L. (1982) Behavior therapy: On roots, contexts, and growth, in G. T. Wilson and C. M. Franks (eds), *Contemporary Behavior Therapy: Conceptual and Empirical Foundations.* New York: Guilford.

Krasner, L. (1985) Book Reviews, *The Behavior Therapist,* **8,** 13.

Krupnick, J., Shea, T. and Elkin, I. (1986) Generalizability of treatment studies utilizing solicited patients, *Journal of Consulting and Clinical Psychology,* **54,** 68–78.

Landis, C. (1937) A statistical evaluation of psychotherapeutic methods, in L. E. Hinsie (ed.), *Concepts and Problems in Psychotherapy.* New York: Columbia Press.

Lang, P. J. (1969). The mechanics of desensitization and the laboratory study of fear, in C. M. Franks (ed.), *Behavior Therapy: Appraisal and Status.* New York: McGraw-Hill.

Lang, P. J. (1977) Imagery in therapy: An information processing analysis of fear, *Behavior Therapy,* **8,** 862–86.

Lang, P. J. (1978) Anxiety: Toward a psychophysiological definition, in H. S. Akiskal and W. L. Webb (eds), *Psychiatric diagnosis: Exploration of biological predictors.* New York: Spectrum.

Lang, P. J. (1980) Foreword, in B. G. Melamed and L. J. Siegel (eds), *Behavioral Medicine: Practical Applications in Health Care.* New York: Springer.

Lazarus, R. S. (1982) Thoughts on the relations between emotion and cognition, *American Psychologist,* **37,** 1019–24.

Lazarus, R. S. (1984) On the primacy of cognition, *American Psychologist,* **39,** 124–9.

Lazarus, R. and Laurier, R. (1978) Stress-related transactions between persons and environment, in L. Pervin and M. Lewis (eds), *Perspectives in Interactional Psychology.* New York: Plenum.

Lehrer, P. M. and Woolfolk, R. L. (1982) Self-report assessment of anxiety: Somatic, cognitive, and behavioral modalities, *Behavioral Assessment,* **4,** 167–77.

Lehrer, P. M. and Woolfolk, R. L. (1984) Are stress reduction techniques interchangeable, or do they have specific effects?: A review of the comparative empirical literature, in P. M. Lehrer and R. L. Woolfolk (eds), *Principles of Stress Management.* New York: Guilford.

Leitenberg, H. (1976) Behavioral approaches to treatment of neuroses, in H. Leitenberg (ed.), *Handbook of Behavior Modification and Behavior Therapy.* Englewood Cliffs, NJ: Prentice-Hall.

Levis, D. J. (1970) Behavioral therapy: The fourth therapeutic revolution? in D. J. Levis (ed.), *Learning Approaches to Therapeutic Behavior Change.* Chicago: Aldine.

Levis, D. (1982) Experimental and theoretical foundations of behavior modification, in A. S. Bellack, M. Hersen and A. E. Kazdin (eds), *International Handbook of Behavior Modification and Therapy.* New York: Plenum.

Leviton, A. (1978) Epidemiology of headache, in *Advances in Neurology (Vol. 19).* New York: Raven Press.

Lewinsohn, R. M., Muñoz, R. F., Youngren, M. A. and Zeiss, A. M. (1978) *Control your Depression.* Englewood Cliffs, NJ: Prentice-Hall.

Liddell, A. (1983a) Professional development, in A. Liddell (ed.), *The Practice of Clinical Psychology in Great Britain.* Chichester: Wiley.

Liddell, A. (1983b) Primary health care, in A. Liddell (ed.), *The Practice of Clinical Psychology in Great Britain.* Chichester: Wiley.

Liddell, A, Hughes, M. and Plotz, T. (1983) The development of a self-controlled exposure programme for clients presenting with phobic and anxiety symptoms. Unpublished Report, Department of Psychology, Memorial University of Newfoundland, St. John's, Newfoundland.

Liddell, A., Mackay, W., Dawe, G., Galitura, B., Hearn, S. and **Walsh-Doran, M.** (1986) Compliance as a factor in outcome with agoraphobic clients, *Behaviour Research and Therapy,* **24,** 217–20.

Liddell, A., May, B., Boyle, M. and **Baker, M.** (1981) How to stimulate GP referrals to a clinical psychology unit, *Bulletin of The Psychological Society,* **34,** 164–5.

Livingston, S. A. (1977) Psychometric techniques for criterion-reference testing and behavioral assessment, in J. D. Cone and R. P. Hawkins (eds), *Behavioral Assessment: New Directions in Clinical Psychology.* New York: Brunner/Mazel.

Lobitz, W. C. and **LoPiccolo, J.** (1972) New methods in the behavioral treatment of sexual dysfunction, *Journal of Behavior Therapy and Experimental Psychiatry,* **3,** 265–71.

Lum, L. C. (1976) The syndrome of habitual chronic hyper-ventilation, in O. W. Hill (ed.), *Modern Trends in Psychosomatic Medicine (Vol.3).* London: Butterworth.

Mackay, W. E. and **Liddell, A.** (1986) An investigation into the matching of specific agoraphobic anxiety response characteristics with specific types of treatment, *Behaviour Research and Therapy,* **24,** 361–4.

Mahoney, M. J. and **Thoresen, C. E.** (eds) (1974) *Self-Control: Power to the Person.* Monterey, CA: Brooks/Cole.

Marks, I. M. (1978) Behavioral psychotherapy of adult neurosis, in S. L. Garfield and A. E. Bergin (eds), *Handbook of Psychotherapy and Behavior Change: An Empirical Analysis,* 2nd edn. New York: Wiley.

Marks, I. M. (1981) Toward an empirical clinical science: Behavioral Psychotherapy in the 1980s, *Behavior Therapy,* **13,** 63–81.

Marks, I. M., Connoly, J., Hallam, R. and **Philpott, R.** (1977) *Nursing in Behavioural Psychotherapy.* Book in Research Series of Royal College of Nursing: Henrietta Street, London WC1.

Marks, I. M. and **Mathews, A. M.** (1979) Brief standard self-rating for phobic patients, *Behaviour Research and Therapy,* **17,** 263–7.

Masters, W. H. and **Johnson, V. E.** (1970) *Human Sexual Inadequacy.* New York: Bantam.

Mathews, A. M. (1978) Fear-reduction research and clinical phobias, *Psychological Bulletin,* **85,** 390–404.

Mathews, A. M., Gelder, M. G. and **Johnston, D. W.** (1981) *Agoraphobia: Nature and Treatment.* New York: Guilford.

Matson, J. L. (1981) A controlled outcome study of phobias in mentally retarded adults, *Behaviour Research and Therapy,* **19,** 101–7.

McMullin, R. and Casey, B. (1975) *Talk Sense to Yourself!* Counseling Research Institute, 8000 West 14th Avenue, Lakewood, CO 80215.

McPherson, I. and Sutton, A. (1981) *Restructuring Psychological Practice.* London: Croom Helm.

Meichenbaum, D. (1975) Self-instructional methods, in F. H. Kanfer and A. P. Goldstein (eds), *Helping People to Change.* New York: Pergamon.

Meichenbaum, D. (1977) *Cognitive-Behavior Modification: An Integrative Approach.* New York: Plenum.

Meichenbaum, D. (1985) *Stress Inoculation Training.* New York: Pergamon.

Meichenbaum, D. and Cameron, R. (1973) Stress inoculation: A skills training approach to anxiety management. Unpublished manuscript, University of Waterloo.

Meichenbaum, D. and Goodman, J. (1971) The nature and modification of impulsive children: Training impulsive children to talk to themselves. Paper presented at the Society for Research in Child Development Conference, Minneapolis, Minnesota, April 1971.

Meyer, V., Levy, R. and Schnurer, A, (1974) The behavioral treatment of obsessive-compulsive disorder, in H. R. Beech (ed.), *Obsessional States.* London: Methuen.

Meyer, V. and Liddell, A. (1975) Behaviour therapy, in D. Bannister (ed.), *Issues and Approaches in the Psychological Therapies.* London: Wiley.

Meyer, V., Liddell, A. and Lyons, M. (1977) Behavioral interviews, in A. R. Ciminero, K. S. Calhoun and H. E. Adams (eds), *Handbook of Behavioral Assessment.* New York: Wiley.

Milby, J. B. Meredith, R. L. and Rice, J. (1981) Videotaped exposure: A new treatment for obsessive-compulsive disorders, *Journal of Behavior Therapy and Experimental Psychiatry,* **12**, 249–55.

Miller, J. G. (1971) The nature of living systems, *Behavioral Science,* **16**, 277–301.

Mineka, S. (1979) The role of fear in theories of avoidance learning, flooding, and extinction, *Psychological Bulletin,* **86**, 985–1010.

Mischel, W. (1968) *Personality and Assessment.* New York: Wiley.

Morrow-Bradley, C. and Elliott, R. (1986) Utilization and psychotherapy research by practicing psychotherapists, *American Psychologist,* **41**, 188–97.

Nelson, R. O. (1983) Behavioral assessment: Past, present, and future, *Behavioral Assessment,* 5, 195–206.

Nelson, R. O. and Barlow, D. H. (1981) Behavioral assessment: Basic strategies and initial procedures, in D. H. Barlow (ed.), *Behavioral Assessment of Adult Disorders.* New York: Guilford.

Norton, G. R., Dinardo, P. A. and Barlow, D. H. (1983) Predicting phobic's response to therapy: A consideration of subjectives, physiological, and behavioural measures, *Canadian Psychology,* 24, 50–8.

Orlinsky, D. E. and Howard, K. E. (1978) The relation of process to outcome in psychotherapy, in S. L. Garfield and A. E. Bergin (eds), *Handbook of Psychotherapy and Behavior Change,* 2nd edn. New York: Wiley.

Öst, L. and Hugdahl, K. (1981) Acquisition of phobias and anxiety response patterns in clinical patients, *Behaviour Research and Therapy,* 19, 439–47.

Öst, L., Jerremalm, A. and Jansson, L. (1984) Individual response patterns and the effects of different behavioural methods in the treatment of agoraphobia, *Behaviour Research and Therapy,* 22, 697–707.

Öst, L., Johansson, J. and Jerremalm, A. (1982) Individual response patterns and the effects of different behavioural methods in the treatment of claustrophobia, *Behaviour Research and Therapy,* 20, 445–60.

Parloff, M. B. (1986) Placebo controls in psychotherapy research: A sine qua non or a placebo for research problem? *Journal of Consulting and Clinical Psychology,* 54, 79–87.

Parloff, M. B., Waskow, I. E. and Wolfe, B. E. (1978) Research on therapist variables in relation to process and outcome, in S. L. Garfield and A. E. Bergin (eds), *Handbook of Psychotherapy and Behavior Change,* 2nd edn. New York: Wiley.

Parsons, O. A. and Hart, R. P. (1984) Behavioral disorders associated with central nervous system dysfunction, in H. E. Adams and P. B. Sutker (eds), *Comprehensive Handbook of Psychopathology.* New York: Plenum.

Paul, G. L. and Lentz, R. J. (1977) *Psychosocial Treatment of Chronic Mental Patients: Milieu versus Social Learning Programs.* Cambridge, MA: Harvard University Press.

Phares, E. J. (1984) *Clinical Psychology Concepts, Methods, and Profession,* revised edn. Homewood, IL: Dorsey.

Philips, C. (1977) Headache in general practice, *Headache,* 16, 322–9.

Philips, C. and Hunter, M. (1981a) The treatment of tension headache – I. Muscular abnormality and biofeedback, *Behaviour Research and Therapy,* **19**, 485–98.

Philips, C. and Hunter, M. (1981b) The treatment of tension headache – II. EMG 'normality' and relaxation, *Behaviour Research and Therapy,* **19**, 499–507.

Pomerlau, O. F. and Brady, S. P. (eds) (1979) *Behavioral Medicine: Theory and Practice.* Baltimore, MD: Williams and Wilkins.

Price, R. H. (1978) *Abnormal Behavior: Perspective in Conflict,* 2nd edn. New York: Holt, Rinehart and Winston.

Rachman, S. (1971a) Obsessional ruminations, *Behaviour Research and Therapy,* **9**, 229–35.

Rachman, S. (1971b) *The Effects of Psychotherapy.* Oxford: Pergamon.

Rachman, S. J. (1978) *Fear and Courage.* San Francisco: Freeman.

Rachman, S. (1980) Emotional processing, *Behaviour Research and Therapy,* **18**, 51–60.

Rachman, S. (1981) The primacy of affect: Some theoretical implications, *Behaviour Research and Therapy,* **19**, 279–90.

Rachman, S. and Hodgson, R. (1974) I. Synchrony and desynchrony in fear and avoidance, *Behaviour Research and Therapy,* **12**, 311–18.

Rachman, S. J. and Hodgson, R. J. (1980) *Obsessions and Compulsions.* Englewood Cliffs, NJ: Prentice-Hall.

Rachman, S. J. and Wilson, G. T. (1980) *The Effects of Psychological Therapy,* 2nd edn. Oxford: Pergamon.

Richardson, F. and Suinn, R. (1973) A comparison of traditional systematic desensitization, accelerated desensitization, and anxiety management training in the treatment of mathematics anxiety, *Behavior Therapy,* **4**, 212–18.

Rimm, D. C. and Master, J. C. (1979) *Behavior Therapy,* 2nd edn. New York: Academic Press.

Rosenthal, T. and Bandura, A. (1978) Psychological modeling: Theory and practice, in S. L. Garfield and A. E. Bergin (eds), *Handbook of Psychotherapy and Behavior Change,* 2nd edn. New York: Wiley.

Ruggles, T. R. and Leblanc, J. M. (1982) Behavior analysis procedures in classroom teaching, in A. S. Bellack, M. Hersen and A. E. Kazdin (eds), *International Handbook of Behavior Modification and Therapy.* New York: Plenum.

Sargent, J. D., Walters, E. D. and Green, E. E. (1973) Preliminary report on the use of autogenic training in the treatment of migraine and tension headache, *Psychosomatic Medicine,* **35,** 129–35.

Schroeder, H. E. and Rich, A. R. (1976) The process of fear reduction through systematic desensitization, *Journal of Consulting and Clinical Psychology,* **44,** 191–9.

Schultz, J. H. and Luthe, E. (1969) *Autogenic Training (Vol. 1).* New York: Grune & Stratton.

Schwartz, G. E. and Weiss, S. M. (1977) Proceedings of the Yale conference on behavioral medicine. (US Department of Health, Education, and Welfare Publication No. (NIH) 78-1424). Washington, DC: US Government Printing Office.

Seligman, M. E. P. (1975) *Helpness: On Depression, Development and Death.* San Francisco: Freeman.

Selye, H. (1976) *The Stress of Life,* 2nd edn. New York: McGraw-Hill.

Shapiro, A. K. and Morris, L. A. (1978) Placebo effects in medical and psychological therapies, in S. L. Garfield and A. E. Bergin (eds), *Handbook of Psychotherapy and Behavior Change,* 2nd edn. New York: Wiley.

Shapiro, D. A. and Shapiro, D. (1982) Meta-analysis of comparative therapy outcome studies: A replication and refinement, *Psychological Bulletin,* **41,** 581–604.

Shepherd, M. and Gruenberg, E. (1957) The age for neuroses, *Millbank Memorial Bulletin,* **35,** 258–64.

Sherrington, C. S. (1947) *The Integrative Action of the Central Nervous System.* Cambridge: Cambridge University Press.

Singh, A. C. and Bilsbury, C. D. (1982) Scaling subjective variables by SPC (Sequential Pair Comparisons), *Behavioural Psychotherapy,* **10,** 128–45.

Singh, A. C. and Bilsbury, C. D. (1984a) Estimating Levels of Subjective Experienced States by a System of Repeated Comparisons. Technical Report No. 84-01. Psychology Department, The General Hospital, Health Sciences Centre, St John's, Newfoundland.

Singh, A. C. and Bilsbury, C. D. (1984b) A Manual for Estimating Levels of Subjectively Experienced States on Discan Scales. Technical Report No. 84-02. Psychology Department, The General Hospital, Health Sciences Centre, St John's, Newfoundland.

Skinner, B. F. (1948) *Walden Two.* New York: MacMillan.

Skinner, B. F. (1953) *Science and Human Behavior.* New York: Free Press.

Sloane, R. B., Staples, F. R. Cristol, A. H., Yorkston, N. J, and **Whipple, K.** (1975) *Psychotherapy versus Behavior Therapy.* Cambridge, MA: Harvard University Press.

Smith, M. L. and **Glass, C. V.** (1977) Meta-analysis of psychotherapy outcome studies. *American Psychologist,* **41,** 752–60.

Stern, R. S., Lipsedge, M. S. and **Marks, I. M.** (1973) Obsessive ruminations: A controlled trial of thought-stopping technique, *Behaviour Research and Therapy,* **11,** 659–62.

Stiles, W. B., Shapiro, D. A. and **Elliott, R.** (1986) Are all psychotherapies equivalent? *American Psychologist,* **41,** 165–80.

Strube, M. J. and **Hartmann, D. P.** (1982) A critical appraisal of meta-analysis, *British Journal of Clinical Psychology,* **21,** 129–39.

Stuart, R. B. (1980) *Helping Couples Change.* New York: Guilford.

Stunkard, A. J. (1984) The current status of treatment for obesity in adults, in A. J. Stunkard and E. Stellar (eds), *Eating and its Disorders.* New York: Raven.

Sturgis, E. T. and **Meyer, V.** (1980) Obsessive-compulsive disorders, in S. M. Turner, K. C. Calhoun and H. E. Adams (eds), *Handbook of Clinical Behavior Therapy.* New York: Wiley.

Suinn, R. (1981) *Manual Anxiety Management Training (AMT).* Ft. Collins, CO: Rocky Mountain Behavioral Sciences Institute, Inc.

Suinn, R. and **Richardson, F.** (1971) Anxiety management training: A non-specific behavior therapy program for anxiety control, *Behavior Therapy,* **4,** 498–510.

Sulzer-Azaroff, B. and **Pollack, M. J.** (1982) The modification of child behavior problems in the home, in A. S. Bellack, M. Hersen and A. E. Kazdin (eds), *International Handbook of Behavior Modification and Therapy.* New York: Plenum.

Sundberg, N. D., Tyler, L. E. and **Taplin, J. R.** (1973) *Clinical Psychology: Expanding Horizons,* 2nd edn. New York: Appleton-Century-Crofts.

Thoresen, C. E. and **Mahoney, M. J.** (1974) *Behavioral Self-Control.* New York: Holt, Rinehart and Winston.

Thorpe, G. L. and **Burns, L. E.** (1983) *The Agoraphobia Syndrome.* Chichester: Wiley.

Truax, C. and **Carkhuff, R.** (1967) *Toward Effective Counselling and Psychotherapy.* Chicago: Aldine.

Tryon, G. S. (1979) A review and critique of thought stopping research, *Journal of Behavior Therapy and Experimental Psychiatry,* **10,** 189–92.

Turner, D. B. and **Stone, A. J.** (1979) Headache and its treatment: A random sample survey, *Headache,* **19,** 74–7.

Ullman, L. P. and Krasner, L. (1969) *A Psychological Approach to Abnormal Behavior.* Englewood Cliffs, NJ: Prentice-Hall.

Upper, D. and Cautela, J. R. (1979) *Covert Conditioning.* New York: Pergamon.

Valentine, E. R. (1982) *Conceptual Issues in Psychology.* London: Allen & Unwin.

VandenBos, G. R. (1986) Psychotherapy research: A special issue, *American Psychologist,* **41,** 111–12.

Watson, J. B. (1914) *Behavior: An Introduction to Comparative Psychology.* New York: Holt.

Watson, J. B. (1919) *Psychology from the Standpoint of a Behaviorist.* Philadelphia: Lippincott.

White, D. R. (1986) Treatment of mild, moderate, and severe obesity in children, *Canadian Psychology,* **27,** 262–74.

Whitehead, A. (1979) Psychological treatment of depression: A review, *Behaviour Research and Therapy,* **17,** 495–509.

Williams, J. M. G. (1984) *The Psychological Treatment of Depression.* New York: Free Press.

Wilson, G. T. (1978) On the much discussed nature of the term 'behavior therapy', *Behavior Therapy,* **9,** 89–98.

Wilson, G. T. and Franks, C. M. (1982) Introduction, in G. T. Wilson and C. M. Franks (eds), *Contemporary Behavior Therapy: Conceptual and Empirical Foundations.* New York: Guilford.

Wilson, G. T. and O'Leary, K. D. (1980) *Principles of Behavior Therapy.* Englewood Cliffs, NJ: Prentice-Hall.

Wolpe, J.. (1958) *Psychotherapy by Reciprocal Inhibition.* Stanford, CA: Stanford University Press.

Wolpe, J., Lande, S. D., McNally, R. J. and Schotte, D. (1985) Differentiation between classically conditioned and cognitively based neurotic fears: Two pilot studies, *Journal of Behavior Therapy and Experimental Psychiatry,* **16,** 287–93.

World Health Organization (1978) Glossary of mental disorders and guide to their classification, in *Manual of the International Statistical Classification of Diseases, Injuries and Causes of Death,* 9th edn. Geneva: WHO.

Yates, A. J. (1958) Symptoms and symptom substitution, *Psychological Review,* **56,** 371–4.

Zajonc, R. B. (1980) Feeling and thinking: Preferences need no inference, *American Psychologist,* **35,** 151–75.

Author index

Subject index